WORLD WAR I
IN COLOUR

WORLD WAR I IN COLOUR

THE DEFINITIVE ILLUSTRATED HISTORY WITH OVER 200 REMARKABLE FULL COLOUR PHOTOGRAPHS

HISTORICAL CONSULTANT
CHARLES MESSENGER

EBURY PRESS
LONDON

2003

I...

...'Warfare' by the

Nugus/M...   ...BLACK AND WHITE.

...L RIGHT TO BE IDENTIFIED

AS THE A...   ...S AND PATENTS ACT 1988.

FIRST PUBLISHED BY EBURY PRESS

RANDOM HOUSE, 20 VAUXHALL BRIDGE ROAD, LONDON SW1V 2SA

RANDOM HOUSE AUSTRALIA (PTY) LIMITED

20 ALFRED STREET, MILSONS POINT, SYDNEY, NEW SOUTH WALES 2061, AUSTRALIA

RANDOM HOUSE NEW ZEALAND LIMITED

18 POLAND ROAD, GLENFIELD, AUCKLAND 10, NEW ZEALAND

RANDOM HOUSE SOUTH AFRICA (PTY) LIMITED

ENDULINI, 5A JUBILEE ROAD, PARKTOWN 2193, SOUTH AFRICA

THE RANDOM HOUSE GROUP LIMITED REG. NO. 954009

WWW.RANDOMHOUSE.CO.UK

A CIP CATALOGUE RECORD FOR THIS BOOK IS AVAILABLE FROM THE BRITISH LIBRARY.

EDITOR: SAM MERRELL

DESIGNER: DAVID FORDHAM

MAPS: RODNEY PAULL

ISBN 0 09 189782 3

PAPERS USED BY EBURY PRESS ARE NATURAL, RECYCLABLE PRODUCTS
MADE FROM WOOD GROWN IN SUSTAINABLE FORESTS.

TYPESET BY MATS, SOUTHEND-ON-SEA, ESSEX

PRINTED AND BOUND IN ITALY BY GRAPHICOM

Contents

ACKNOWLEDGEMENTS

The film footage, from which the illustrations in this book come, was originally researched and collected in black-and-white by Nugus/Martin Productions for its series *The Century of Warfare*.

It was supplied by the following archives: The Imperial War Museum, London; Reuters Television Library, London; the US National Archive, Washington D.C.

The footage was then colourised by a team project-managed by Sony Pictures International, and used as the basis for the series *World War I in Colour* which was first broadcast in the United Kingdom by Five.

Individual frames from the colourised footage were then selected for this book and transferred using an advanced computer programme which allowed them to be cleaned and downloaded for use on the printed page.

The Introductions to each chapter have been adapted from *The Century of Warfare* originally written by Charles Messenger.

CHRONOLOGY

1914

28 JUNE	Archduke Franz Ferdinand assassinated.
1 AUGUST	Germany declares war against Russia.
3 AUGUST	Germany declares war against France.
4 AUGUST	Germany invades Belgium; Britain declares war against Germany.
14 AUGUST	Battle of the Frontiers (French offensive into Alsace and Lorraine).
23 AUGUST	Battle of Mons
26–29 AUGUST	Battle of Tannenberg (Eastern Front: German victory over Russia)
5–9 SEPTEMBER	Battle of the Marne
12 OCTOBER–11 NOVEMBER	First Battle of Ypres

1915

10–13 MARCH	Battle of Neuve Chapelle
25 APRIL	Allied troops land at Gallipoli.
22 APRIL–25 MAY	Second Battle of Ypres
7 MAY	Sinking of the *Lusitania*.
9–25 MAY	Battle of Aubers Ridge
22 MAY	Italy declares war against Austria-Hungary.
31 MAY	First Zeppelin raid on London.
25 SEPTEMBER–13 OCTOBER	Battle of Loos
28 NOVEMBER	Austria and Bulgaria defeat Serbia.
13 DECEMBER	British and French troops occupy Salonika, Greece. Also in December, Haig replaces Sir John French as British commander-in-chief.

1916

8 JANUARY	Gallipoli evacuation completed.
21 FEBRUARY	Battle of Verdun begins.

31 May	Battle of Jutland
4 June	Start of Brusilov's Russian offensive in Galicia.
1 July–13 November	Battle of the Somme
August	Von Hindenburg and Ludendorff become chiefs of German staff.
15 September	First use of the tank, during the Somme.
December	Lloyd George replaces Asquith as British prime minister.

1917

1 February	Germany begins unrestricted submarine warfare.
6 April	United States declares war against Germany.
9–14 April	Battle of Arras
10 April	Canadians take Vimy Ridge.
15 May	Pétain replaces Nivelle as French commander-in-chief, following mutiny in the French army.
7 June	British take Messines Ridge (following detonation of 19 huge mines).
26 June	First units of the US army arrive in France.
31 July	Third Battle of Ypres begins.
24 October	Austrians defeat the Italians at Caporetto.
6 November	British capture Passchendaele Ridge.
7 November	Bolshevik Revolution in Russia.
20 November	Battle of Cambrai (the first battle where a large number of tanks are used – 378).
15 December	Russo-German armistice

1918

3 March	Germany and Russia sign the Treaty of Brest-Litovsk.
21 March	Germans launch a massive offensive against the British and French.
14 April	Foch appointed commander-in-chief of the Allied armies.
15 July	Germans begin their last offensive against the French.
8 August	British attack at Amiens (Ludendorff described this as 'the Black Day for the German army').
26 September	Widespread Allied offensives on the Western Front, including US assault in the Meuse-Argonne sector.
23 October	Germany accepts US President Wilson's Fourteen Points for peace.
9 November	Kaiser Wilhelm II abdicates and flees to Holland.
11 November	Armistice signed by the Germans.

INTRODUCTION

For those who lived through it, World War I became the 'Great War'. They knew it had been a watershed in history – and life could never be the same again. It was an unprecedented war in almost every way: the worldwide scope of the conflict; the size of the armies involved; the horrific scale of the casualties; the total involvement of civilians; the terrifying advances in technology which fundamentally changed how wars were fought in the future.

It was also the first war to be widely filmed. The movie camera had been invented barely 20 years before and for the first time people could see the harsh realities of war – the fighting, suffering and death. But the images could only be shown in black and white, because that was the only technology available at the time. Yet, of course, the men who fought and died lived in a world of colour – the sky was blue, the grass was green, the mud brown and the blood red.

Today for the first time the technology exists to turn what was filmed – often at great personal risk – into colour, and this was done for the television series *World War I in Colour* on which this book is based. Meticulous research into every detail of the colour of the uniforms, weaponry and battlefields, has enabled the producers to re-create the vivid reality of that Great War. For the first time the modern viewer and reader can witness what the men who fought in this terrible conflict would really have seen. The colour images give an intimacy and immediacy to those distant horrific events.

World War I was a titanic clash of five great empires, which utterly destroyed three and fatally weakened the others. Between 1914 and 1918 some 65 million men were involved in the fighting, whether as willing volunteers or reluctant conscripts. Ten million died in battle and over 20

million were dreadfully wounded – either physically or mentally. There were few families, on both sides, who did not lose someone – sons, husbands, fathers and friends. Almost an entire generation of young men was lost.

During the nineteenth century the Western world had experienced an extraordinary industrial and technological revolution. Economies had developed at an incredible pace and populations had grown enormously. Every aspect of human affairs had been changed – not least the methods of waging war. Two wars in particular, the American Civil War (1861–65) and the Franco-Prussian War (1870–71), had given some indication of what was to come, but World War I was the first war in which all the developments of the Industrial Revolution came together in a new and awesomely frightening way.

Everyone who fought in the war – from the humblest soldier, sailor or airman to the most senior general and admiral – had to come to terms with and respond to the unforeseen ways in which these enormous changes transformed the tactics of warfare and the reality of the battlefield. They saw the birth of aerial combat both on land and at sea; submarine warfare; the first use of the internal-combustion engine to bring mobility to the battlefield; radio-telegraphy, which would transform battlefield communications; and the appearance of chemical warfare.

Few anticipated the way in which the armies of the Western Front ground to a halt, and how barbed wire, machine-guns and massed artillery brought a stalemate – the horror of trench warfare – in which millions were to die in apparently hopeless and futile assaults. Few recognized how technology would then provide the means by which this stalemate in the trenches could be broken in the final few months of the war. A revolutionary new dimension was added to warfare with the swift development of aerial combat. The Wright brothers had only made the first powered flight in 1903, but by the end of the war all the main forms of combat known today – dogfighting, interception, ground attack, reconnaissance, strategic bombing – had been devised and deployed. At sea, new inventions like the submarine and the aircraft carrier showed how the long reign of the mighty battleship as Queen of the Seas had come to an end.

For civilians it was a total war on a scale never before experienced. Whole populations mobilised either to go to the Front or to work in the industries on which the new mass warfare depended. Food had to be rationed, every aspect of life was affected, and the first air raids on cities brought ordinary people into the front line as never before.

So appalling was the carnage of World War I that many could not believe that Europe would ever suffer another war, and it was called 'the war to end all wars'. Yet so great were the new forces it released and so deep the bitterness it caused that a second, even more cataclysmic, world war was unleashed barely 20 years later.

This is the background of the war which this book and the television programmes it accompanies attempt to re-create. For the first time World War I can be seen in its true colours, just as it was seen by the people who suffered through it.

WORLD WAR I
WAS WAR ON A SCALE

NEVER KNOWN OR IMAGINED BEFORE

1 THE WORLD GOES TO WAR
1900–1914

*I kissed my mother and cleared everything up
and I said goodbye mam and I don't think I shall
ever see you again.*

HUBERT WILLIAMS:
ROYAL FLYING CORPS, 1896–2002

Queen Victoria, who had reigned over Britain and its empire for nearly 65 years, died on 22 January 1901. Her death marked the end of an era of relative peace, especially in Europe, which had not witnessed a war for 30 years. It was the longest period of stability that the region had enjoyed for hundreds of years. Queen Victoria's going would, however, mark the beginning of a period of growing uncertainty and tension. Just over a decade later Europe would be plunged into a war that would last for over four long years and claim some nine million lives.

In 1900 the main focus of world affairs still lay with the major European powers. In the east was the huge Russian Empire, which was ruled by the autocratic Tsar Nicholas II. Russia had a large and growing industry but, compared with western Europe, it was backward and inefficient. Its workers, who were poorly paid and housed, seethed with discontent.

Neighbouring Austro-Hungary was a shadow of its former self, especially since its defeat by Prussia in 1866. Here another emperor, the elderly Franz Joseph, ruled over an uneasy combination of Austrians, Hungarians and Poles, and looked to dominate the polyglot races of the Balkans to the south. His northern neighbour Germany was the young

and growing giant of Europe. A collection of kingdoms and principalities under the military domination of Prussia, Germany had only been united at the conclusion of Prussia's shattering defeat of France in 1870. Under the ambitious Kaiser Wilhelm II, a great-nephew of Queen Victoria, Germany had a large and powerful army and a rapidly expanding and efficient industry.

France, a republic since the abdication of the Emperor Napoleon III after the débâcle of 1870, lived for one thing: the recovery of its eastern provinces of Alsace and Lorraine, ceded to Germany after that war. The French Army was therefore kept in a high state of readiness. France also sought to enlarge and consolidate her colonial possessions in Africa and Indo-China.

Britain, with King Edward VII now its titular head, had an empire which was the envy of the other powers. Enlarged under Queen Victoria, it now covered one-sixth of the globe. Its greatest benefit was trade, with raw materials being imported and manufactured goods exported to the world. In order to guard its far-flung empire Britain relied mainly on the Royal Navy, then by far the largest fleet in the world.

Outside Europe there were two emerging powers. The United States of America was just entering a boom time, which would see its gross national product almost triple between 1897 and 1914. This was accompanied by a rapid rise in immigration. Determination never to be influenced by Europe had given rise to a policy of isolation. Nonetheless, as a result of a war fought with Spain in 1898 over Cuba, America had, in 1900, the beginnings of an empire. Not only did the war gain Cuba its independence, it also gave the United States Puerto Rico, Guam and the Philippines.

The other emerging power was Japan. Until the American Commodore Matthew Perry visited in 1853, the country had been a closed society locked in a medieval time warp. Such was the impact he had on the Japanese that they suddenly developed a desire to adopt Western technology and to become a major trading nation. The transformation was swift and dramatic. In 1894 Japan went to war with China and gained her first overseas possession, Korea. The Japanese aim was to become the major power in the Far East.

Empire was, however, to be one of the seeds of the coming conflict. For the western European nations imperial concerns centred on Africa. Britain, France, Germany, Belgium, Italy, Portugal and Spain all possessed territory on that continent. Kaiser Wilhelm II dearly wanted to expand his colonial territory and was envious of the size of Britain's territories. He was delighted when war broke out in South Africa in 1899 between the British and the Boers, who wanted to break away and set up their own republic. The Boers initially inflicted a series of embarrassing defeats on the British Army, and it took the British almost three years to bring about a Boer surrender.

German support for the Boers chilled relations with Britain. The Kaiser also clashed with the French over Morocco in north-west Africa. In 1905 he made a contentious visit to Morocco and six years later, when the Sultan asked for French help to crush mutinous tribesmen, the Germans sent a gunboat to Agadir on the Atlantic coast in order to dissuade the French from staying on. War seemed possible, especially when Britain declared support for France, and only skilful diplomacy brought about a peaceful resolution.

War, however, did come to North Africa in 1911. Libya, part of the decaying Turkish Ottoman empire, was coveted by Italy, which had a number of settlers there. On the pretext of their bad treatment by the Turks, the Italians invaded, seizing the ports of Tripoli, Benghazi, Tobruk and Derna, before becoming embroiled in guerrilla warfare against the Arabs in the interior. The conflict spread to other Turkish territories, especially in the Aegean, where the Italians seized a number of islands. This war saw the first use of aircraft, with bombs being dropped on dissident Arab encampments in Libya.

On the other side of the world colonial rivalry caused war between Russia and Japan. The bone of contention was Korea. The Russians were colonising Manchuria and wanted to extend their influence into Korea. Failing to achieve a diplomatic solution, the Japanese landed troops in northern Korea in spring 1904. They forced the Yalu river and entered Manchuria, driving the Russians north towards Mukden and away from their naval base at Port Arthur on the China Sea, which they besieged. In mid-October, a large Russian fleet set out from the Baltic to relieve Port Arthur. The base, however, fell in January 1905, and the Russian fleet was now ordered to break through to Vladivostok, its key Siberian port in the North Pacific. Eventually, in May 1905, the fleet arrived in the Tsushima Straits, which separate Korea from Japan. The Japanese fleet was waiting and, to the amazement of the world, blew the Russian vessels out of the water. Of its thirty-eight warships only three arrived in Vladivostok.

This humiliating defeat came as the last straw to the discontented Russian people. Unrest grew and included a mutiny of the crew of the battleship *Potemkin* of the Black Sea Fleet. It culminated in a general strike in October, which forced the Tsar to concede to the demand for a national legislative assembly, the Duma. But essentially his autocratic rule remained unchallenged. The 1905 Revolution was, however, a clear warning.

The Japanese naval victory in the Tsushima Straits helped to nurture another seed of conflict. The Germans saw that to be a world power they needed not just empire and a large economy, but also a mighty navy. In 1897, they decided to create a fleet to match Britain's. Under Admiral von Tirpitz, a massive ship-building programme was initiated. At this time a new type of all-big-gun battleship came into being, the dreadnought, named after the first of its kind, HMS *Dreadnought*, which was launched in early 1906. This made all existing capital

ships obsolete. The result was the dreadnought race between Britain and Germany. German efficiency soon cut the average build-time from three to two years. This created a scare in Britain, and an increasing number of dreadnoughts, each class with ever larger guns, was laid down. Other nations – the Americans, French, Italians and Russians – also began building, raising tensions still further.

Two armed camps in Europe had also been created. In 1879 Germany and Austro-Hungary had formed an alliance to counter possible aggression by France or Russia. When Italy joined three years later, this became known as the Triple Alliance. In response, France and Russia formed a pact in 1894. Italy, however, muddied the waters, by pledging in 1902 that she would never fight France in exchange for a free hand in Libya. Britain, traditionally suspicious of France and of Russia's designs on Afghanistan and northern India, stayed out of Continental entanglements, but did ally herself with Japan in 1902 to divert Russian attention. But Germany's growing industrial might and threat to traditional British markets forced Britain to rethink her policy. In May 1903 Edward VII visited Paris, so paving the way for the Entente Cordiale, signed the following year.

Finally, in 1907, came the Anglo-Russian Entente. All the pieces positioned on the chessboard.

It was, however, in the Balkans that the real trouble lay. Once part of the Ottoman Empire, by 1900 there were five independent states in the region – Bulgaria, Greece, Montenegro, Romania and Serbia. Furthermore, the provinces of Bosnia and Hercegovina, although nominally still under Turkish control, were garrisoned by Austrian troops. In 1908 there was a coup d'état in Turkey and a group of reforming army officers, the Young Turks, came to power. Austria, fearful that this would strengthen the Turkish position in Bosnia and Hercegovina, promptly annexed them. This brought an outcry from neighbouring Serbia, since Bosnia had a large Serb population. Russia, now taking a deep interest in the Balkans because of the large Slav population there, supported Serbia, but Germany supported Austria. Serbia therefore climbed down and turned her attention to Macedonia to the south. Serbia also formed alliances with its neighbours and the Balkan League was formed. In October 1912, encouraged by Turkey's problems with Italy over Libya, the League declared war on her. By May 1913 the Turks had been driven out of Europe, apart from toeholds in the Dardanelles and around Constantinople. Serbia's successes in the Balkans fostered both her own self-confidence and a

(ABOVE) Crowds cheer as Austro-Hungarian troops pile into the railway wagons taking them to fight Serbia. Once Austria had declared war, the intricate system of European alliances meant that the major powers were drawn inexorably into a continent-wide conflict.

nationalism among the Slavs of Bosnia-Hercegovina strong enough to plunge the whole of Europe into war.

On 28 June 1914 the Archduke Franz Ferdinand, heir to the Austro-Hungarian throne, was making an official visit to the Bosnian provincial capital of Sarajevo with his wife. As they were en route from the railway station someone threw a bomb at their car. It missed its target and did not explode and the couple arrived safely at the town hall. However, later in the day their driver took a wrong turning and halted in front of a café where their would-be assassin was sitting. This time he did not fail and shot them both. Police immediately arrested the assassin, Gavril Princip, who turned out to be a Bosnian farmer's son and a member of the Young Bosnia independence group. While Austria was unable to prove it, suspicions grew that Serbia was behind the assassination. Therefore, on 23 July, after consulting with Germany, the Austrians delivered an ultimatum to Serbia. She must stop all propaganda over Bosnia-Hercegovina and allow Austro-Hungarian officials into Serbia to conduct a judicial investigation into the outrage. The Serbians were prepared to accept all demands apart from this last, and proposed that the matter go to arbitration. At the same time, though, they began to mobilise their forces. This prompted Vienna to declare war on Serbia on 28 July, doing so, for the first time in history, by telegram.

The fuse was now lit. Berlin, faithful to its ally, warned St Petersburg that any form of Russian mobilisation in support of Serbia would be countered by German mobilisation and war. In spite of French pleas, Russia began a partial mobilisation against Austro-Hungary. Then, on 30 July, Austrian guns began to bombard the Serbian capital Belgrade and full Russian mobilisation was ordered. German mobilisation and a declaration of war against Russia followed immediately. But the German plans for war against the Entente were geared towards avoiding a two-front war at all costs. They took advantage of the likely slow Russian mobilisation by aiming to defeat France first. The French ambassador to Berlin was therefore asked if France would stay neutral. He replied that France would consult her interests, and on 1 August the French began to mobilise. That was sufficient for the German government. The troop trains started to roll westward and war was declared against France two days later.

The final piece of the jigsaw was Britain. Because her ententes with France and Russia were only understandings she initially took a neutral stance. But the realisation grew that an all-dominant Germany on the Continent would not be in her interests. On 4 August German troops entered Belgium and the British government invoked an 1839 treaty on

Belgian neutrality. An ultimatum was given to Berlin to withdraw. This was rejected, the Germans terming the treaty 'a mere scrap of paper'. Thus that night Britain also found herself at war.

As the nations deployed their forces, each did so according to a carefully prepared plan. The Germans owed theirs to Count Alfred von Schlieffen, Chief of the Great General Staff for 14 years from 1891. Recognising the dangers of having to fight Russia and France at the same time, and realising that France would mobilise very much more quickly than her ally, he decided to deliver an early knock-out blow in the west and then deal with Russia. Assuming that the first French move would be to regain Alsace-Lorraine, he envisaged a huge turning movement sweeping through the Low Countries and then swinging west of Paris in order to seize the French capital and attack the bulk of the French armies from behind. Von Schlieffen's successor, Helmut von Moltke, was not wholly happy with the plan and gradually amended it to effect the sweep through Belgium alone. He also strengthened the forces in Alsace-Lorraine at the expense of the right wing of the wheel. These amendments would cost Germany dearly.

Pre-war theorists had identified the French Army's greatest strength as a moral one, its *élan* or dash, which made it more effective in attack than in defence. Hence the French planned to take to the offensive at

the outset and, as von Schlieffen had rightly surmised, against Alsace-Lorraine. The French Army was formidable. It had learnt from its shortcomings of 1870, could call upon combat-hardened colonial troops from North Africa and also had the best field artillery of its time, the quick-firing 75-mm gun, the *soizante-quinze*.

Unlike the Continental armies, the British Army was all-volunteer. It was therefore smaller and much of it was committed to the defence of empire. The French therefore looked primarily to the might of the Royal Navy. Even so, it was agreed that a small force, initially just four divisions and some cavalry, would be sent across the Channel at the outbreak of war. The Army had learnt much from the Boer War and was thoroughly professional, especially its infantry, who were trained to fire fifteen aimed shots per minute. An all-Regular army, however, suffers from a lack of trained reserves. Those that were available were largely used to bring Regular units up to strength. Field Marshal Lord Kitchener, who was appointed minister of war, planned to recruit an all-volunteer force from civilians, but it would be some months before Kitchener's New Armies, as they were called, would be ready.

The German wheel crossed into Belgium and closed on the forts of Liege. The forts were bombarded into submission and on 14 August the Germans entered the Belgian capital, Brussels, and then began to swing south towards the French frontier. Meanwhile, the small Belgian army withdrew westward towards Antwerp.

On the same day that Brussels fell, French troops crossed into Lorraine, pushing back the German outposts. So began the Battle of the Frontiers, which was marked by French attack and German counter-attack. It was German heavy artillery and machine-guns which told, and the French fell back, having suffered 300,000 casualties in two weeks of fighting.

Not a tree stands. Not a square foot of surface has escaped
mutilation. There is nothing but the mud
and the gaping shell holes; a chaotic wilderness of shell holes,
rim overlapping rim; and, in the bottom of many,
the bodies of the dead . . .

CAPTAIN ROWLAND FIELDING

I marvel myself sometimes how human nerves can stand
the strain of our existence; day after day, night after night,
hour after hour, a heavy shell falling every few minutes
within a few yards of you, shaking the ground beneath you,
half stunning you with the crash of explosion.

CAPTAIN ROWLAND FIELDING

To the north-west one French army and the small British Expeditionary Force faced the bulk of the German forces. On 23 August at Mons, a small Belgian town just north of the French border, the Germans faced the firepower of the British infantry for the first time, suffering heavy losses. In danger of being outflanked, however, the British and French were forced to withdraw south. Now began an exhausting two weeks' retreat, which took the Allies back to east of Paris.

But all was not well with the Schlieffen Plan. Troops had to be detached to besiege Namur and Antwerp. Congestion made resupply difficult and the troops were becoming exhausted. Worse, the wheel began to contract and swing east, instead of west of Paris, as it pursued the Franco–British forces. Also, the two westernmost armies found it difficult to keep in contact with one another, and von Kluck's First Army, on the western tip, nudged ever closer to its neighbour. The French hastily gathered another army in the Paris area. When the Germans were across the River Marne, this army, with a large fleet of Paris cabs helping to move it to the front, attacked the Germans in the flank. Von Kluck was caught off balance and pulled back northward. Soon the withdrawal became general. The Miracle of the Marne had done for the Schlieffen Plan, and both sides were now almost exhausted. When the Germans reached the Aisne, the next major river-line to the north, they dug in. Half-hearted Allied attempts to shift them failed and by mid-September both sides had taken what was to be a brief pause for breath.

The relatively small German forces in East Prussia (in present-day northern Poland) had been ordered to remain on the defensive until they received reinforcements from the west. Austro-Hungary had different ideas, however. Although embroiled in Serbia, Conrad von Hoetzendorf, the Austrian chief-of-staff, also planned to attack the vulnerable salient created by Russian Poland from the south, believing that the Germans would attack it from the north. The Austrian Army was, however, an imperfect instrument. Not least, it suffered from a lack of cohesion due to its multi-ethnic make-up, which did not help military efficiency.

The Russians, too, had an offensive strategy, also based on the Polish salient. One army would strike north from it and another from the east to cut off and destroy the German forces in East Prussia and advance on Berlin. Simultaneously, other armies were to strike south into Austrian Galicia so as to trap the Austrian forces there north of the Carpathian mountains. The Russian Army was the largest in Europe, capable of mobilising six million men, but it was cumbersome. A poor railway system meant that mobilisation and deployment were slow. Corruption and incompetence were rife among senior officers. The rank and file were largely illiterate peasantry, but they did have courage and endurance.

The Austrian attack on Serbia did not go well and things went little better in Galicia. The Russian and Austrian armies, both bent on attack, literally blundered into one another north and east of Lemberg. The Austrians came off slightly the worse and retreated some 100 miles westward before withdrawing behind the River Wislaka.

In East Prussia, however, events were more dramatic. Just after dawn on 17 August cavalry of Rennenkampf's Russian First Army crossed East Prussia's eastern border. Three days later Rennenkampf attacked the main body of the German Eighth Army at Gumbinnen. The Russian right wing was driven back, but in the centre the Germans panicked and von Prittwitz, the army commander, decided to withdraw. But Rennenkampf did not follow up his success and halted. Samsonov, commanding the Russian Second Army, thinking that a decisive victory had been achieved began his advance from the south. At this point von Prittwitz was replaced by Paul von Hindenburg, a retired officer, with Erich Ludendorff, who was commanding an

infantry brigade in front of the Liege forts, as his chief-of-staff – a combination that was to become formidable.

Von Hindenburg and Ludendorff arrived on 23 August. Rennenkampf had still not moved, while Samsonov was continuing to advance slowly northward. The two German generals found that von Prittwitz's deputy chief-of-staff, Colonel Max Hoffman, had already prepared a plan to strike at Samsonov's exposed left wing and were also well aware of the Russians' intentions thanks to their practice of transmitting uncoded messages on their few primitive radios. On 26 August the Germans attacked and, after four days, destroyed the Russian Second Army, its commander committing suicide. Von Hindenburg chose the name of Tannenberg for his victory after a town in the area where the Teutonic Knights were defeated by the Poles, Russians, and others 500 years earlier.

Von Hindenburg now turned on the Russian First Army and, during the Battle of the Masurian Lakes, drove it out of East Prussia and back across the River Niemen, inflicting 60,000 casualties. Thus, by mid-September, all the initial attempts by each side to mount a decisive offensive on the Eastern Front had failed, as they had in the west. Although the Germans had won two convincing victories they could not exploit them until they received reinforcements from the west. They were also aware that so far only a small portion of Russia's military strength had been deployed.

Outside Europe other clashes with the Germans had broken out. Japan, seeing the opportunity to enlarge her growing overseas possessions, invoked her 1902 treaty with Britain and offered help in reducing Germany's one foothold in China, Tsingtao on the Yellow Sea coast. In September a Japanese force, with two British battalions, landed and laid siege to it, supported by an Anglo-Japanese naval squadron. Tsingtao fell in early

One of the most brilliant battles in the history of the world had been fought [Tannenberg]. . .
Germany and Austria-Hungary rejoiced.
The world was silent.

GENERAL ERICH LUDENDORFF,
MEMOIR

*In those days your brains – what shall I say – wasn't
developed enough to realise what war was
and everybody said it'll be over by Christmas.
Now Christmas came and it wasn't.*

HARRY PATCH:
DUKE OF CORNWALL'S LIGHT INFANTRY,
BORN 1898

November, and the German islands in the Pacific were also quickly occupied by Japanese, New Zealand and Australian forces. But Germany's Pacific naval squadron escaped to the South Atlantic, where it was to create problems for the Royal Navy.

In southern Africa a campaign was launched by South African troops to seize German south-west Africa, but there were problems to be resolved before this could get under way. Hardline Afrikaaners in South Africa, still resentful of the British, attempted a revolt to prevent South Africa from fighting on their side. The vast majority of the South African Defence Forces remained loyal to the Crown, however, and quickly crushed the opposition. The advance into the German colony could now begin and was soon making headway against the comparatively weak German colonial forces.

Closer to home, Britain's Mediterranean Fleet suffered an embarrassing setback when two German warships, the *Goeben* and the *Breslau*, due to be delivered to the Turkish Navy, successfully evaded all attempts to intercept them. Their safe arrival in Constantinople encouraged Turkey, which already enjoyed close relations with Germany, to side with the Central Powers.

These campaigns, and others about to open, began to give the war its global aspect. The decisive fronts, however, were in Europe. In both east and west the initial war plans had largely failed, and it was becoming clear that the earlier widespread belief that the war would be over by Christmas one way or the other was very optimistic. The question now was what to do next.

IT WAS A TIME OF EMPIRES, THE THREE LARGEST RULED BY MEN WHO WERE COUSINS – DIRECTLY DESCENDED FROM BRITAIN'S QUEEN VICTORIA.

(ABOVE) Tsar Nicholas II takes part in a religious procession. A weak and indecisive man, who was easily influenced – particularly by his wife Alexandra who is beside him – the Tsar nevertheless saw himself as God's Annointed, an absolute ruler who must be obeyed without question. On the other side of the Tsar is his son and heir the haemophiliac Tsarevich Alexei, being carried by a servant.

(TOP RIGHT) The majority of Russia's 170 million population still lived in almost medieval conditions. Serfdom had only been abolished in 1861, and most peasants still regarded the Tsar as their 'Little Father', an almost God-like being.

(BOTTOM RIGHT) The Tsar blesses his generals. Ultimately his rule depended on the loyalty of them and their troops, and the work of a massive secret police force. The standing army of 1.4 million – mostly conscripts – was by far the largest in the world, with more than 4 million reservists.

A united nation since only 1871, Germany was the rising force
of Europe, ruled by the ambitious Kaiser Wilhelm II.
Germany formed an alliance with the much older empire of
Austria-Hungary. Together these central powers now dominated
the heart of Europe.

THE TWO EMPIRES WHOSE ALLIANCE DOMINATED CENTRAL EUROPE WERE AN EXTRAORDINARY CONTRAST – ONE NEW AND PURPOSEFUL, THE OTHER CENTURIES-OLD AND DECREPIT.

(ABOVE LEFT) Kaiser Wilhelm II of Germany in his favourite role – as warlord of the most respected and feared army in Europe. His empire had only been formed in 1871 and the volatile and arrogant Kaiser was desperate to make up for lost time, using his superb army to dominate continental Europe.

(ABOVE) The Austro-Hungarian Emperor Franz Joseph with the ladies of his court in Vienna. In 1914 he was 83, and grappling with the problems of holding together a sprawling 800-year-old empire which was being torn apart by ethnic and religious rivalries.

KAISER WILHELM II'S BOMBAST AND AGGRESSION HAD ONE UNWELCOME
RESULT — A RIVAL ALLIANCE TO CONTROL HIS AMBITIONS.

(ABOVE) Britain's King Edward VII at a shoot. Although he cultivated the image of a sporting monarch with a liking for the ladies, Edward played a key role in ending the centuries-old enmity between Britain and France. His visit to Paris in 1903 was a triumphant success, and led to the Entente Cordiale and an alliance of the two countries with Russia.

(TOP RIGHT) A street scene in 'Gay Paree' – Paris was widely regarded as the cultural capital of the world. France was unique in being the only republic among the major European powers, and the only other one with an overseas empire anywhere as large as Britain's. Its standing army of 567,000 men was backed by 3.5 million trained reservists.

(BOTTOM RIGHT) Edward VII's successor George V rides in state as Emperor of India at the Delhi Durbar in 1911. Britain's empire covered one-sixth of the earth's land surface. To protect it, Britain had built by far the largest navy in the world but only a small professional army, which was mainly equipped for colonial defence.

WHEN THE SPARK CAME AFTER MORE THAN 30 YEARS OF IMPERIAL
RIVALRIES IT WAS SMALL AND UNEXPECTED. AT FIRST NO ONE TOOK MUCH
NOTICE OF AN ASSASSINATION IN THE TROUBLESOME BALKANS.

(TOP LEFT) Archduke Franz Ferdinand was visiting Sarajevo, capital of the Austro-Hungarian province of Bosnia, to observe army manoeuvres. These were intended to warn Serbia not to encourage any independence movements.

(BOTTOM LEFT) Gavril Princip, a 19-year-old student and member of the Young Bosnia independence group, is arrested moments after shooting the Archduke and his wife.

(ABOVE) The Archduke's coffin is carried in state during its journey back to Vienna. After years of trouble in the Balkans many in the Austro-Hungarian government saw his murder as an ideal opportunity to reassert the empire's power.

ONCE THE AUSTRIANS HAD DECIDED TO PUNISH SERBIA, THE ALLIANCES OF THE GREAT POWERS TURNED A SIDESHOW INTO A CONTINENTAL WAR.

(ABOVE) Austro-Hungarian troops set off for war. Once Russia had seen that fellow Slavs were under threat it felt obliged to mobilise in support. Germany, the ally of Austro-Hungary, was obsessed by the danger of a war on two fronts – against both Russia and its Western ally France.

(RIGHT TOP AND BOTTOM) Small but loyal Germans parade as their country mobilises. German strategy was dictated by the plan developed by General Alfred von Schlieffen in the 1890s. To avoid the danger of war on two fronts Germany must first defeat France and then switch back by rail to deal with the slower-mobilising Russians.

*There was an atmosphere then of almost jubilation, now we're going
to fight and do something useful. We didn't realise
what war really involved.*

ARTHUR HALESTRAP MBE:
ROYAL ENGINEERS,
BORN 1898

WHILE THE FRENCH WERE EAGER TO REVENGE
THEIR DEFEAT BY PRUSSIA IN 1870, MOST
BRITONS WENT ON THEIR SUMMER HOLIDAYS
LITTLE SUSPECTING WHAT WAS ABOUT TO HAPPEN.

(ABOVE LEFT) French troops mobilising. Eager to recover the 'lost' provinces of Alsace and Lorraine, there was little popular enthusiasm to give way to German demands that France guarantee not to support its ally Russia.

(ABOVE) The first units of the British army march through London to Victoria Station on their way to France. Britain had undertaken to send four divisions of its small army to support France immediately war was declared on Germany.

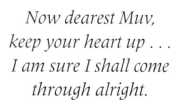

*Now dearest Muv,
keep your heart up . . .
I am sure I shall come
through alright.*

2ND LIEUTENANT
CYRIL RAWLINS

Volunteers flocking to enlist in London and being marched off to barracks in their civilian clothes. It was the half-forgotten commitment to defend Belgian neutrality which tipped Britain into war. Almost half of Britain's small professional army of 247,000 men was stationed abroad, and it had only 200,000 trained reservists. The small Territorial Army of 268,000 men was trained and equipped solely for home defence. But Britain's public, after almost a century of peace, was eager to help 'plucky little Belgium' and the flood of volunteers meant that conscription was unnecessary.

BRITAIN'S ARMY WAS TOO SMALL AND
UNEQUIPPED TO COPE WITH THE SORT OF WAR
INTO WHICH IT WAS UNEXPECTEDLY THRUST.

(ABOVE) The British Expeditionary Force arrives in France. All the men of this first 'Contemptible Little Army' – as the Kaiser described it – were highly trained professionals. German troops were shocked by the speed and accuracy of the British rifle fire – 15 aimed shots per minute – and were convinced that they must have far more machine-guns than the two per battalion which were available.

THE SCHLIEFFEN MASTERPLAN HAD SENT THE BULK OF THE GERMAN ARMY
IN A MASSIVE OUTFLANKING MOVEMENT TOWARDS PARIS. BUT THE FRENCH
COMMANDERS SEEMED BLIND TO THE DANGER.

(ABOVE) German infantry in their *pickelhaub* helmets march through Belgium in the summer heat. The sheer scale of Schlieffen's plan had panicked his successor Helmut von Moltke and he reduced it. Even then the great wheel proved difficult to control.

(TOP RIGHT) French cavalry displaying its customary Napoleonic *élan*. Obsessed by his disastrous offensive into Alsace and Lorraine, the French commander Joseph Joffre ignored the danger looming up behind him until it was almost too late.

(BOTTOM RIGHT) Paris taxis take troops to the front only 20 miles from Paris. It was General Galieni, commander of the Paris garrison, who gathered a makeshift army and launched it against the exposed German flank, thus winning 'the Miracle of the Marne'.

THE UNEXPECTED SPEED OF RUSSIAN MOBILISATION
CAME CLOSE TO UPSETTING THE FUNDAMENTAL
ASSUMPTION OF VON SCHLIEFFEN'S PLAN.

(TOP AND BOTTOM LEFT)
Cossack cavalry move into East
Prussia only two weeks after
war is declared. Two Russian
armies invaded from the northeast and the south. Separated
by almost 100 miles of thick
forests, lakes and swamps, they
were too far apart for mutual
support. Even worse, their
commanders hated each other
and were determined not to co-
operate in any way.

(ABOVE) German horse
artillery deploy their guns. The
Germans were outnumbered
more than two to one. After a
brief skirmish against the
northern Russian army the
German commander panicked
and tried to abandon the
province. He was sacked, but
his deputy chief-of-operations,
Colonel Max Hoffman, saw an
opportunity to defeat each
Russian army in turn.

(TOP) Machine-gunners of a *Landwehr* reserve battalion use a Maxim 7.92-mm machine gun to harass the enemy. Leaving only token forces in the north, the new German command team sent an army corps over 150 miles by rail to the flank of the southern Russian army. This was advancing through thick forests around the town of Tannenberg – completely unaware of any threat.

(MIDDLE) A German infantry firing line – they are equipped with the standard 7.92-mm *Gewehr* 08 rifle with a five-round magazine. As the Russians straggled ever deeper into the Tannenberg forest, the German armies closed around it.

(BOTTOM) Then one army corps thrust forward behind them to cut them off while two more struck down from the north. The confused Russian forces broke and ran in panic.

Colonel Hoffman's tactical genius and the decisiveness of the new German commanders in East Prussia – Generals Paul von Hindenburg and Erich Ludendorff – combined to win one of history's greatest victories – the Battle of Tannenberg.

More than 60,000 Russians were made prisoner and at least that number were killed at Tannenberg. The Germans were then able to use their superior organisation to move back to the north. A few days later, in the Battle of the Masurian Lakes, they forced the northern Russian army to retreat. Thanks to these victories, never again during World War I did the Russians threaten German territory.

THESE YEARS WOULD PRODUCE A NEW AND DEADLY EXPRESSION — GOING OVER THE TOP

2 BLOOD AND MUD

Trench Warfare In The West 1914–1918

What was a man's life in this wilderness whose vapour was laden with the stench of thousands upon thousands of decaying bodies? . . . Chivalry here took a final farewell.

LIEUTENANT ERNST JUNGER,
MEMOIR

Although the Germans' initial offensive on the Western Front had failed, they were still determined to deal France a knock-out blow. East of Paris the front may have solidified, but north of the River Aisne and right up to the Belgian coast, there existed a virtual vacuum. If the Germans could outflank the Allies they could still achieve a decisive result. The Allies, determined to build on their recent success outside Paris, thought the same.

So began the month-long Race to the Sea. The two sides marched northward in parallel, and every attempt to outflank each other was foiled. Eventually, in mid-October, the race ended in a dead heat at the Channel coast. Still determined to achieve an early decisive victory, the Germans decided to punch a hole in the thin Allied line, at Ypres.

In October 1914, Ypres was at the base of a salient jutting into the German lines. The northern face was held by the French and the southern by the British. It was on the latter that the Germans were to concentrate their efforts. For three weeks they threw everything they had against the stretched Allied defences. At one point the Germans sent young half-trained volunteers into the attack. Incapable of advancing other than shoulder-to-shoulder, they were mown down. The Germans themselves called it the Massacre of the Innocents. The

line held, but only just, and such were its casualties that the old British Regular Army could be said to have found its grave here. Ypres also confirmed that the machine-gun and magazine rifle had tipped the scales in favour of defence. Ypres was also the final German effort to win a quick victory in the West, now they went on the defensive.

Both sides, exhausted and bemused, dug in, and soon there was an unbroken line of trenches which stretched from Switzerland to the North Sea.

Trench warfare meant new skills had to be learnt – patrolling and sniping, laying barbed wire, trench construction – and new weapons began to appear. Trench mortars, capable of lobbing high-explosive bombs into trenches, and grenades became primary trench weapons. The machine-guns of the day were soon found to be too cumbersome and a new, lighter breed of automatic weapon, like the Lewis gun used by the British and the French Chauchat, began to appear. Opposing front-line trenches were sometimes as little as 100 yards apart, and any visible movement by day attracted the enemy's fire. Night therefore became the time for work. Patrols crept across no-man's land to check on the opposing trenches and find out how strongly they were held. Food, ammunition, water and other supplies had to be brought up on men's backs through the communication trenches that stretched back from the front line.

The Allied politicians and commanders spent the winter of 1914–15 working out how they could break the deadlock. The Westerners argued that the decisive blow must come on the Western Front. The Easterners, led by one Winston Churchill, First Lord of the Admiralty, stated that since there was stalemate in the West the Allies should look elsewhere to apply pressure. The result of this was the campaign in the Dardanelles, designed to knock Turkey out of the war and then threaten the Central Powers. Opened in the spring of 1915, it quickly degenerated into another deadlock.

In February 1915 the French commander-in-chief, Joseph Joffre, issued a directive. The French were to strike three simultaneous blows, in Artois and Champagne, the shoulders of the great German salient, and also in Lorraine. The British contribution was to be a limited attack in support of the French effort in Artois.

These attacks set the pattern for the next three years. An opening artillery barrage, an advance across no-man's land, struggling through the wire in front of the enemy trenches, then bloody hand-to-hand fighting. At this point the surviving attackers needed to quickly reorganise themselves for the inevitable counter-attack, but cries for reserves often went

If any man tells you he went over the top and he wasn't scared, he's a damn liar.

HARRY PATCH:
DUKE OF CORNWALL'S LIGHT INFANTRY,
BORN 1898–

unheeded. A telephone cable would be run back from the captured trenches, but too often it was cut by shell fire. The runner was usually the only means of communication, but many never made it back across no-man's land. The result so often was that the pitifully small numbers of surviving attackers were left to fight it out on their own and perished.

French and British commanders thought that the German trench systems needed to be bombarded for much longer. However, field guns like the French '75' and British 18-pounder were not powerful enough to cause major trench destruction. As for heavier artillery, the French and the British had relatively few pieces and these were often old-fashioned and inaccurate. The Germans, however, had a large amount of heavy artillery from the outset. Worse, the British especially had almost expended all their stocks of ammunition by spring 1915 and guns had to be rationed to as little as two rounds per day. It took a newspaper magnate, Lord Northcliffe, to galvanise the British government into taking urgent action to set up more ammunition factories under the newly appointed minister for munitions, David Lloyd George. Many of those who came to work in these factories were women.

Towards the end of April 1915 the Germans introduced a new and terrible weapon – gas. The scene was the embattled Ypres salient and the type of gas was chlorine. The Germans, who had only been experimenting, were not in a position to take full advantage and launch a major attack, but, even so, it was only thanks to desperate efforts by the recently arrived Canadians, who urinated in their handkerchiefs and used them as gas masks, that a major disaster was avoided. Later in 1915 the Germans unveiled another new and equally terrible weapon, the flamethrower.

In the early summer of 1915 the French launched another big attack in Artois after a four-day bombardment by over 1200 guns, while the British attacked at Aubers Ridge and Festubert. Once again, the fog of war meant that initial success could not be exploited in time, and, in any event, the Germans were even better dug-in than they had been earlier in the year.

Casualties continued to mount on both sides. The Germans and French carried on calling up conscripts, but the British still resisted compulsory military service and looked largely to Kitchener's volunteers of the New Armies, who began to arrive at the front in spring 1915.

Joffre remained mesmerised by the huge salient bound by Artois and Champagne. Once again he called for major attacks in these sectors, with the British supporting the Artois offensive. The assaults were mounted on 25 September after a four-day bombardment, with the British attacking first at Loos. They managed to break through the German lines, but the commander-in-chief, Sir John French, held his reserves too far back. The opportunity for a breakthrough was thus lost. This cost French his command and he was replaced by Sir Douglas Haig. The French offensive in Artois also gained little, while that in Champagne showed early promise, but also failed. These offensives cost the Allies 250,000 casualties and the Germans 140,000.

The Allies drew up their plans for 1916 in December. They called for simultaneous offensives on the Eastern and Western Fronts and also by the Italians, who had entered the war in May 1915. Joffre had now given up his attempts against the shoulders of the German salient and resolved on an offensive against its nose and astride the River Somme, with the British, whose strength in France was steadily growing, attacking north of the river and the French to the south. But the Germans, too, were planning. Their efforts against Russia during 1915 had not met with decisive success. Erich von Falkenhayn, war minister and chief-of-staff, decided to strike once more in the West. While he regarded Britain as the true enemy, he decided to attack her 'best sword', France, and to do so in such a way as to bleed her armies to death. He therefore chose one of France's ancient fortresses, which were so much a symbol of her history.

The fortress town of Verdun stood at the centre of two concentric lines of forts. Many of the forts' guns had been removed to more active sectors, however, and little effort had been made to maintain the defences. When the Germans attacked on 21 February 1916, they quickly disorganised the defenders, capturing key forts. For a time it seemed that there was little to stop the Germans from seizing Verdun itself, but the French clung on. Reinforcements began to arrive, but their movement and that of supplies was hampered by the fact that there was only one road available. It took superhuman efforts to keep La Voie Sacrée (the Sacred Road), as it became known, open, but the French were determined to hang on and Verdun became a symbol of French doggedness. Not until December did the battle finally end. By then each side had suffered some 360,000 casualties.

The Allies were still determined that their 1916 offensive should go ahead. However, the attack astride the Somme was now primarily a British effort. On 24 June 1916 over 2000 guns began pounding the German lines on a 20-mile front. Twenty-two British and eight French infantry divisions massed for the attack. A week later, on the morning of 1 July, the attack went in.

The day was one of disaster. Only the French below the Somme reached their first day's objectives. To their north the British suffered nearly 60,000 casualties. The bombardment had not caused significant damage to the German trenches and so the lines of advancing men were easy targets for the machine-guns.

Perennial poor communications meant that it was some time before the generals appreciated what had happened, but even then they could not stop. They could not let down their Russian and Italian allies and had to take some of the pressure off Verdun. Names like Thiepval, Gommecourt, High Wood, Montauban and Beaumont Hamel became synonymous with blood and anguish. It was not until November that the British finally halted their attacks. In four and a half months they advanced a maximum of seven miles at a cost of over 400,000 casualties.

No matter how dangerous the errand, the runner on duty never wants calling twice. He will pick up his rifle and be off, often to his death.

CAPTAIN ROWLAND FIELDING,
LETTER TO HIS WIFE

If the first Battle of Ypres had been the graveyard of the British Regular Army, then the Battle of the Somme was undoubtedly that of Kitchener's volunteers.

The winter of 1916–17 on the Western Front was one of the coldest. The ground remained frozen hard until April and sickness in the trenches rose alarmingly. The two sides could make good some of their devastating losses, with the British now finally having to adopt conscription.

The failures of 1916 resulted in new faces taking over the reins of power. Lloyd George replaced Asquith as prime minister in December 1916. Horrified by the Somme losses, he wanted to get rid of Haig as the British commander in France, but was unable to do so as Haig's reputation still stood high. In France, Joffre was replaced by Robert Nivelle as commander-in-chief. Germany's von Falkenhayn suffered for his failure at Verdun and was succeeded by Paul von Hindenburg and Erich Ludendorff.

The Germans realised that they were stretched too thin on the Western Front and so decided to shorten their line. They spent the winter constructing formidable defences, involving much concrete and primarily in front of the British sector. These were called the Siegfried Line by the Germans and the Hindenburg Line by the Allies.

The British had spent most of 1915 and the first half of 1916 developing a tracked armoured vehicle capable of crossing trenches and overcoming barbed wire. The result was the tank, so called because, for security reasons, early models were transported by train under the cover of being water tanks for the Middle East. Forty nine tanks made their battlefield debut on 15 September 1916 during the Somme offensive with mixed results, but their potential was clear.

The tank and the attrition of the German armies in France and Flanders convinced Nivelle that the Allies could quickly break through the German defences. Anglo-French forces would pin down the Germans north of the Oise, while the main blow would be struck in the hilly and wooded Chemin des Dames sector immediately south of the Oise. After a prolonged and pulverising bombardment by nearly 3000 guns the French would attack.

The offensive was to be mounted in April, but it was the Germans who moved first when they began to pull back to their new defence line in March. This took the Allies by surprise, and their follow-up was slow off the mark and not helped by numerous German booby traps. This withdrawal seemed to negate the attack north of the Oise, but Nivelle was insistent that the offensive should go ahead.

*You couldn't just stand there and wait for ever,
something had to be done. . . . it was up to the Allies
to try and break through this great log jam.*

MALCOLM BROWN:
HISTORIAN, IMPERIAL WAR MUSUEM,
INTERVIEWED FOR THE PROGRAMME

The British attacked at Arras on 9 April. The first day saw a spectacular success when the Canadians captured the dominant Vimy Ridge. Otherwise there were few gains. Sixty tanks were used, but many fell victim to machine-guns firing armour-piercing ammunition, while others became bogged down.

The Chemin des Dames attack was supposed to start on the same day as that at Arras, but was postponed because it was felt that the guns had not inflicted enough damage. The French did not begin their attack until 16 April, after the guns had been firing for nine days. The Germans were well aware of the plan and had three well-fortified defence lines. Consequently, the French suffered heavy casualties from the outset and gained little ground.

After their sufferings at Verdun, Chemin des Dames proved too much for many French troops. At the beginning of May unrest began to develop with more and more units refusing to carry out pointless attacks. The French Government sacked Nivelle and replaced him with Henri Pétain, hero of Verdun. The rot had now spread to no less than 16 army corps, and Pétain realised that the only way that the army could be nursed back to health was by going on the defensive.

The French mutinies, and the fact that German submarines were in danger of severing Britain's lifeline across the Atlantic, made spring 1917 a grim time for the Western Allies. There was, however, one ray of hope. On 6 April the United States entered the war.

Pétain was concerned that the Germans would take advantage of the weakened state of the French Army and attack. He therefore turned to Douglas Haig and his five British armies. They must attack to divert German attention. In June 1917, a limited attack was to be mounted in

order to secure the dominant Wyteschaete–Messines ridge south of Ypres. Then, towards the end of July, the main attack would be launched, its objective being Bruges. Once this had broken through the German lines, an amphibious assault, together with a simultaneous land attack along the coast, would turn the German flank.

The attack on the Wyteschaete–Messines ridge was meticulously planned and made extensive use of underground mines. The British had tried a huge mine one year earlier on the first day of the Somme offensive. From January 1916 the British tunnellers had been hard at work under the Wyteschaete–Messines ridge. In the early hours of 7 June no less than 19 mines were exploded under the ridge; the noise of the detonation was heard in south-east England. The troops then attacked and quickly overwhelmed the numbed defenders.

This model attack boded well for the main offensive, which was to begin at the end of July, with the amphibious landings scheduled for a week later during the first August high tide. Thirty British and four French divisions would attack out of the Ypres salient on a 15-mile front, and the offensive was to be preceded by a barrage that would continue for 15 days, the longest bombardment yet witnessed on the Western Front. The attack went in on the morning of 31 July and the first results were promising, but in the afternoon it began to rain, and it rained for the next ten days. The artillery had upset the delicate drainage system in Flanders and further shelling and rain quickly turned the battle area into a quagmire. Hopes of an early breakthrough faded and the amphibious landing was cancelled. Time had to be allowed for the ground to dry out, which gave the Germans a breathing space. Every time the attacks were renewed the rain quickly followed, and before long another drawn-out battle of attrition had developed.

The landscape was reduced to mud and shell holes filled with water in which many men drowned. Still, the attacks continued, for German attention had to be maintained on Flanders, especially so since it was becoming clear that Russia was on the point of collapse and the Germans might switch forces westward for an attack on the still fragile French. Eventually, the beginning of November found the British at their last gasp struggling for the Passchendaele ridge, just under six miles from the original start-line. Forty one square miles of mud had been captured in fifteen weeks of fighting. Each square mile cost some 10,000 casualties.

The end of Third Ypres, as the battle was called, did not quite mean an end to active operations in 1917. The Tank Corps was determined to prove that the tank could be a war-winner. They selected a piece of terrain far removed from the mud of Ypres – the rolling chalklands east of the Somme battlefield in the region of Cambrai. Led in person by General Hughes Elles, the Tank Corps commander, 378 tanks crashed across no-man's land at dawn on 20 November without any preliminary bombardment. Followed by six divisions of infantry, the tanks broke through the surprised Germans and had advanced up to five miles by nightfall. It seemed as though the long-hoped-for breakthrough had been achieved, but next day only 40 tanks were fit for action. By the end of November an advance of a further two miles had been made, but then the Germans launched a major counter-attack, driving the British almost back to their start-line.

Thus the close season on the Western Front began a little later than in earlier years. The October 1917 revolution in Russia meant that she was out of the war, and it was known that the Germans were now switching additional troops to the West. With the Americans still having little more than token forces in France, and the British and French exhausted by the 1917 offensives, there was no option but to go on the defensive and await the inevitable German attack.

The Germans themselves had been perfecting a new form of assault, which had been tried both on the Eastern Front and in the Cambrai counter-attack. It was spearheaded by specially trained teams of stormtroops, who were to infiltrate as quickly as possible to the depth of the enemy's defences. Short preliminary barrages, deploying a large number of gas shells, were designed not so much to destroy trench systems as to isolate them from the rear and disrupt communications.

The first German blow was to be struck against the British, and aimed to isolate them from the French and force them northward with their backs to the English Channel. Two factors operated in the Germans' favour. Firstly, Lloyd George, appalled at the slaughter during Third Ypres, decided to put a partial brake on reinforcements being sent to France. This left Haig with a fighting strength less than it had been a year earlier, although he had agreed with the French, who were also desperately short of manpower, to take over an additional 25 miles of front southward across the River Oise. Secondly, a thick mist played into the hands of the stormtroops when they attacked at dawn on 21 March 1918 on a 64-mile front. In the south the overstretched Fifth Army was soon in retreat and fell back some 15 miles. Ferdinand Foch was formally appointed Allied Generalissimo in order to improve

the coordination of operations. By now the German thrust showed signs of slowing. The drive was finally brought to a halt short of Amiens, all the gains made by the British on the Somme in 1916 having been lost, and more territory besides.

Hindenburg and Ludendorff now turned to the French. At the end of May they attacked at Chemin des Dames, hoping to draw off the French reserves so that they could attack the British once more. Within four days they had reached the Marne, an advance of 30 miles. Here the defences were too strong and they had outrun their supplies. Among the defenders on the Marne were two American divisions, who acquitted themselves well in a counter-attack at Belleau Wood. This was the first US action on the Western Front. The threat of increasing American strength caused the Germans to become desperate. They attacked again on 9 June, this time along the line of the Oise. The French, however, were becoming wise to the German tactics and allowed some penetration before counter-attacking from the flanks.

The Germans had now incurred some 800,000 casualties in their four drives, and their strength and morale were on the wane. Nevertheless, Ludendorff was bent on one more attempt to snatch a decisive victory. Massing 52 divisions, he struck in Champagne on 15 July. The French main defences were set well back, and when the stormtroops came up against them they were out of supporting artillery range. Momentum was lost and once more the French, with American support, attacked in the flanks, tanks leading the way. The German gamble, aimed at forcing a decision in the West before the Americans became too strong, had failed. Now it was to be the turn of the Allies to attack once more.

WAR ON THE WESTERN FRONT

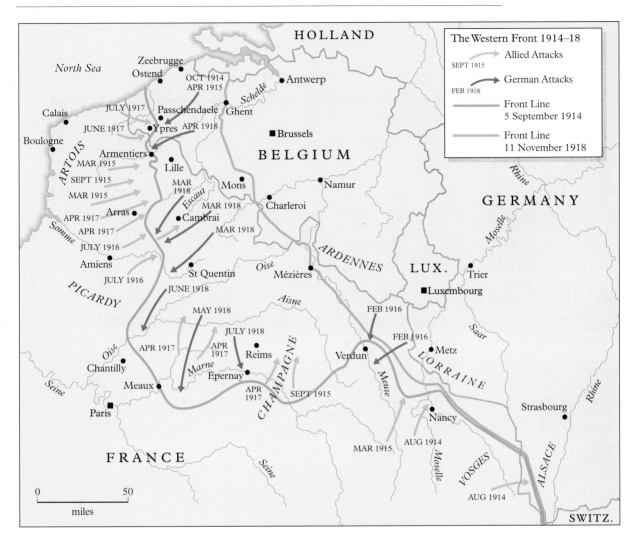

The Western Front 1914–18

SEPT 1915 — Allied Attacks

FEB 1918 — German Attacks

—— Front Line 5 September 1914

········ Front Line 11 November 1918

The attack in the west would be one of the most difficult operations in history I was perfectly sure, and I did not hide the fact. The German nation, too, would have to give it all it had.

GENERAL ERICH LUDENDORFF,
MEMOIR

FOLLOWING THE GERMAN DEFEAT AT THE BATTLE OF THE MARNE, BOTH
SIDES RACED NORTH TRYING TO OUTFLANK EACH OTHER. SOON AN
UNBROKEN LINE OF TRENCHES STRETCHED OVER 400 MILES FROM THE
NORTH SEA TO THE SWISS BORDER.

(TOP LEFT) The ruins of Ypres in October 1914. The Germans tried unsuccessfully to capture the town and lost thousands of troops in frontal attacks over open ground, cut down by British machine-guns.

(BOTTOM LEFT) A British shell explodes during the preliminary bombardments for the battle of Neuve Chapelle in February 1915. Allied commanders were convinced that intense barrages would solve the trench stalemate.

(ABOVE) British troops in a waterlogged dugout during the winter of 1914–15. Unable to make any headway against the machine-guns and barbed wire of the enemy's defences, both sides now dug in.

By the spring of 1915, the British army had virtually run out of ammunition. The government was forced to begin an urgent programme of building new munitions factories.

(Above) A British Mark 7 naval gun in action during the spring of 1915. By then ammunition reserves were exhausted and some units could only fire two rounds a day.

(Right) Girls in an ammunition factory, 1915. Women were virtually the only new source of labour and were essential for the war effort. World War I brought a revolution in the workplace as women proved that they could perform just as well as men. Conditions in the munitions factories were awful. Working with cordite caused rotting teeth, severe headaches and sometimes unconsciousness. TNT caused rashes, swellings and yellowed skin.

'THERE IS NO ARMY', WAS FIELD MARSHAL LORD KITCHENER'S FIRST
REACTION WHEN APPOINTED SECRETARY OF STATE FOR WAR.
IT TOOK HEROIC EFFORTS FOR BRITAIN TO BUILD A MASS ARMY FOR
WARFARE ON A CONTINENTAL SCALE.

(ABOVE) A recruiting officer
drumming up volunteers at a
meeting in London. On 7 August
Kitchener had appealed for a
'First Hundred Thousand' men.
Such was the patriotism that
gripped the nation that numbers
were no problem, and by
Christmas 1914 more than a
million men had joined up.

*It is a great and glorious thing
to be going to fight for
England.*

2ND LIEUTENANT
CYRIL RAWLINS

(TOP) Men of the 'Kitchener Army' preparing to go to the Front. Morale was high – even after the massive losses suffered in the battles of 1915. Volunteers continued to flood in – more than a million in 1915 and another million in 1916. It was only then that Britain had to introduce conscription to keep up the flow.

(MIDDLE) Australian troops marching to the Front. The contribution of Britain's empire was on a similar scale to that of the mother country. By the end of the war, Canada had contributed over 620,000 men, Australia more than 412,000, and New Zealand 128,000 – the highest in proportion to population, after Britain.

(BOTTOM) British gunners load an ammunition limber during the four-day preliminary barrage in preparation for the attack at Loos in September 1915. It was part of a joint offensive with the French, in which little was gained at the cost of 250,000 casualties.

AS 1916 OPENED, A NEW GERMAN COMMANDER, ERICH VON FALKENHAYN,
PLANNED TO LURE THE FRENCH ARMY INTO A KILLING GROUND WHERE IT
WOULD BE BLED TO DEATH.

(ABOVE) French dead lie amid the shambles of the Verdun battlefield. Over 360,000 men were killed, and the German 'mincing machine', as it was known, came very close to success. But at a terrible cost, for almost as many Germans died during the battle.

(TOP RIGHT) Exhausted French troops mass for a counter-attack. Verdun lasted from 21 February to 15 December, and three-quarters of the French army were sucked into the fighting.

(BOTTOM RIGHT) French wounded being evacuated. For much of the battle, there was only one road – La Voie Sacrée – into Verdun. Up this all French reinforcements had to struggle and the wounded be carried out – under constant artillery bombardment.

THE DISASTROUS ALLIED ASSAULTS OF 1915 BROUGHT NEW COMMANDERS,
BUT THEIR ONLY SOLUTION TO THE STALEMATE WAS MORE OF THE SAME.

(TOP LEFT) Field Marshal Sir Douglas Haig, who took command of the British Expeditionary Force in December 1915. He was convinced that only by 'wearing-out' the enemy – however long it might take and however many casualties it might involve – would the war move into its final phase of 'a final decisive blow'.

(BOTTOM LEFT) A British field-gun battery on exercise before the battle. Three divisions of cavalry were waiting behind the front line to exploit the breakthrough which was confidently expected.

(ABOVE) The bombardment on the Somme begins. The British had massed more than 2000 guns – almost 170 for every mile of front – and, in an eight-day bombardment, these fired over 1.7 million rounds. The infantry were assured that all the German barbed wire and other defences would be annihilated, and all they would have to do was stroll across.

WITHIN MOMENTS OF
THE TROOPS LEAVING
THEIR TRENCHES, IT
WAS CLEAR THAT THE
BARRAGE HAD NOT
WORKED – THE
BRITISH ARMY WAS
ABOUT TO EXPERIENCE
THE SINGLE MOST
BLOODY DAY IN ITS
HISTORY.

(ABOVE) 'Going over the top'.
The artillery barrage has lifted
and the moment of truth
arrived as the men set off on
the short walk across no-man's
land to the enemy's trenches.

(RIGHT) Early morning on
1 July 1916. As zero hour
approaches for the Somme
offensive, British infantry move
up to the front line. They are
wearing the steel helmet which
had been introduced during
1915, and are armed with the
trusty Lee-Enfield .303-inch
rifle with a five-round
magazine that remained in use
until the 1960s.

(TOP) The German defences had remained virtually intact, and the British infantry faced withering machine-gun fire from the moment they set off.

(MIDDLE) By the end of the day, the British had suffered more than 57,470 casualties and captured only a few enemy positions. But with more and more of the French army being sucked into the 'meat grinder' at Verdun, Haig could see no alternative but to keep on launching fresh attacks.

(BOTTOM) A machine-gun team during one of the 330 counter-attacks with which the Germans blocked any hope of an Allied breakthrough. They are wearing the characteristic 'coal scuttle' helmet which was just being introduced, and which became a symbol of German military power in both world wars.

THE MEN OF BRITAIN'S 'NEW ARMY' WERE EAGER 'TO DO THEIR BIT'. BUT THEY HAD BEEN TRAINED ONLY TO ADVANCE IN LINE – PERFECT TARGETS ON A PERFECT SUMMER'S DAY.

(ABOVE) Bringing in the wounded. The huge Somme offensive ground on until November, causing over 400,000 British and 200,000 French casualties for the gain of less than seven miles.

Although they were on the defensive for most of the battle, the courage and incredible ferocity of the German counter-attacks meant that they eventually lost almost as many men as the Allies.

THE DESPERATE BATTLE ON THE SOMME – HAIG'S 'WEARING OUT FIGHT' IN
WHICH HUNDREDS OF THOUSANDS OF TROOPS WERE SLAUGHTERED – HAS
COME TO SYMBOLISE THE HORROR OF WORLD WAR I.

(ABOVE) A British officer
slumped in death – probably
cut down by shrapnel. During
1916–17, a young front-line
officer on either side could
expect to last only a few weeks.
By the end of 1916, the British
Empire forces had suffered
over a million casualties.

(TOP RIGHT) A British
'Tommy' helps bring back a
wounded German prisoner
during the Somme. Although it
is the sacrifice of the British
and French troops during the
offensives which is generally
remembered, the Germans
were suffering almost as much.

(BOTTOM RIGHT) Piles of
German dead in a shell crater.
The Germans found the
growing power and accuracy of
Allied artillery a constant and
deadly threat. In the end, more
men were to be killed by
artillery during World War I
than by rifles or machine-guns.

*I always said a prayer . . . some of those lads used to laugh
at me, but I always asked God
to make me fight like a man and bring
me back safe and sound.*

ARTHUR BARRACLOUGH:
DUKE OF WELLINGTON'S REGIMENT,
BORN 1898

ALTHOUGH IT SEEMED IMPOSSIBLE TO BREAK THE STALEMATE, THERE WERE POINTERS TO WAYS IN WHICH IT MIGHT BE DONE.

(ABOVE LEFT) British troops 'debus' from a motor truck. Both sides realised that the internal combustion engine offered a revolution in mobility. In 1914 the British had 1485 motor vehicles, by 1918, 121,170.

(ABOVE) A British infantryman firing a Lewis gun. Not only had the number of machine-guns increased enormously by the middle of the war, but lighter and more portable types were introduced.

THE ENTHUSIASM WITH WHICH THE SOMME OFFENSIVE HAD BEGUN WAS REPLACED BY A GRIM DETERMINATION TO SEE THE JOB THROUGH. AS CHARLES CARRINGTON PUT IT PROUDLY: 'WE WERE NOT INTIMIDATED BY THE WAR OF ATTRITION . . .'.

Hope we shall be successful on Saturday morning July 1st at dawn when you are all fast asleep . . . I have got to go over with the first batch. I can imagine how everything looks at home.

PRIVATE ARTHUR HUBBARD:
LETTER TO HIS SISTER, 29 JUNE 1916

(LEFT) British troops moving up for an attack on the Somme.

(TOP) Troops resting during a lull. One of the major problems on the battlefield was that once they had left their trenches there was virtually no way of communicating with them reliably – radios were too cumbersome, telephone lines could get broken and runners could be shot. Commanders were effectively cut off from their leading troops.

(MIDDLE) The winter of 1916–17 was one of the coldest on record. This helped to ensure that the Allies were not ready to strike early in 1917 and seize the chance to deal the exhausted Germans the 'final decisive blow' Haig longed for.

(BOTTOM) British gunners struggle through the spring mud. The Allies' hopes of going on the offensive early were also thrown into disarray when the Germans pulled back several miles in February to the heavily fortified Hindenburg Line, leaving a vacuum where they had planned to attack.

AS 1917 BEGAN, A NEW FRENCH COMMANDER WAS CONFIDENT THAT ONE MORE PUSH WOULD LEAD TO VICTORY. HE DID NOT ALLOW FOR THE EXHAUSTION OF HIS OWN MEN.

(TOP LEFT) General Robert Nivelle, the charismatic general who took command of France's army at the beginning of 1917. Once his spring offensive stalled, his troops began to refuse to attack again.

(BOTTOM LEFT) A French *poilu* bringing in German prisoners. Most French troops did not desert their posts but the British were forced to bear the brunt of the fighting for the rest of 1917.

(ABOVE) Decorating the colours of a French regiment which had not mutinied. It took months for General Philippe Pétain, who replaced Nivelle on 15 May 1917, to restore the morale of the French army.

THE KILLING GROUND ON DURING 1917, BUT ATTEMPTS WERE BEING MADE
TO FIND WAYS OF BREAKING THE STALEMATE.

(ABOVE) British miners digging a mine under the Wyteschaete–Messines Ridge during 1916. Attempts to use mechanical diggers were unsuccessful and most of the work in the 2000-foot (600-metre) long tunnels was done by hand.

(TOP RIGHT) An officer listens for enemy counter-mining. There was a constant danger of a sudden attack. Sometimes the Germans would try to detonate charges under British tunnels, and occasionally tunnels would meet and desperate fights would ensue.

(BOTTOM RIGHT) Connecting up the firing wire. On 7 June 1917 at 0320 hours, 19 mines – over 1 million tons of high explosive – were blown. Most of the German front line ceased to exist, but the British were unable to follow up quickly enough to break through.

ARTILLERY WAS TO
DOMINATE THE
BATTLEFIELD OF 1918,
AND IT WAS DURING
1917 THAT THE
GUNNERS FULLY
DEVELOPED THEIR
SKILLS.

(LEFT) The British now had an adequate number of guns and shells. They had also realized that bombardment would not destroy the enemy's forward defences sufficiently for a breakthrough. Instead communications and supply dumps were targeted as well.

(ABOVE) A British 12-inch railway gun. In addition to the 'creeping barrage', which could advance just ahead of front-line troops, the gunners were experimenting with predicted ranging, which meant that targets were plotted ahead of time and a sudden, surprise bombardment unleashed.

IT WAS THE DEVELOPMENT OF THE TANK WHICH WAS TO HAVE THE MOST LASTING EFFECT ON THE FUTURE OF LAND WARFARE.

(TOP LEFT) British Mark IV tanks training on Salisbury Plain. They weighed about 30 tons, carried an eight-man crew, could achieve about 3.5 miles an hour, and were armed either with two 6-pounder guns or machine-guns.

(BOTTOM LEFT) Infantry cheering the tanks during the Battle of Cambrai on 20 November 1917. They had been introduced in small numbers towards the end of the Battle of the Somme, but achieved little.

(ABOVE) At Cambrai 378 Mark IVs were used en masse in conjunction with a sudden barrage and helped the infantry to break clear through the German lines. But by the next day most of the tanks had broken down and the Germans were able to recover.

THE YEAR 1917 ENDED AS IT HAD BEGUN – IN
EXHAUSTION AND MUD. BUT EACH SIDE HAD
REASONS FOR BOTH HOPE AND FEAR.

(ABOVE) A Mark IV 'Female'
tank – with machine guns –
grinds through the mud.
Despite many disappointments,
the tank and the new methods
of artillery bombardment at last
seemed to offer the Allies a way
of breaking the stalemate if
they could find the will.

(TOP RIGHT) Bringing out
wounded to a field ambulance.

(BOTTOM RIGHT) A transport
moving through the shattered
landscape. Both sides were
having grave difficulties finding
sufficient men, but America
had now entered the war on
the side of the Allies, while
Russia had given up, and the
Germans could move men from
the east.

(LEFT) President Woodrow Wilson with newsmen shortly after he had brought his country into the conflict.

(RIGHT) General John Pershing, leader of the American Expeditionary Force. Before 1917 his main military experience had been leading a punitive expedition to hunt down the Mexican rebel leader Pancho Villa.

(BELOW) The first American infantrymen embark for Europe. In 1917 the United States had only 110,000 men.

(TOP RIGHT) Pershing speaking to his troops in France. By December 1917 there were still only 140,000 of them in France and only one division was at the front – in a quiet sector.

(BOTTOM RIGHT) The enormous industrial power of the United States now gave the Allies the promise of unlimited material for their armies.

TWO YEARS ON THE DEFENSIVE HAD TAKEN THEIR TOLL ON THE GERMAN ARMY – THE TROOPS WERE DESPERATE TO GO ON THE OFFENSIVE.

(ABOVE) A German machine-gun team in action. As 1917 ended, the German army was experimenting with new tactics which they believed might end the stalemate. Lightly armed mobile troops who would use surprise to break through the enemy's lines.

(TOP RIGHT) German prisoners bringing in British wounded. The carnage of 1916 and 1917 had had different effects on the two armies. The Germans had lost the experienced core of their superb army, while the British volunteers and conscripts had become a more professional force.

(BOTTOM RIGHT) British troops burying German corpses during a lull in one of the assaults with which Germany tried to bring the War to an end in the first half of 1918, before the build-up of American troops became too great.

MILITARY COMMANDERS BEGAN TO REALIZE THAT FLIGHT MIGHT BE USEFUL FOR WAR

3 ACES HIGH
Air Warfare 1914–1918

*A glorious death! Fight on and fly on to the last drop of
blood and the last drop of petrol . . . a death for a knight . . .*

BARON MANFRED VON RICHTHOFEN

When Europe went to war in 1914, the heavier-than-air flying
machine had only become fact just a few years previously.
Armies and navies, however, quickly realised that the aircraft could be
useful as a means of reconnaissance and could possibly fulfil other roles
as well. Indeed, during its first use in war, in the conflict between the
Italians and Turks in Libya in 1911, the Italians used aircraft for
directing artillery fire and for bombing attacks, as well as for
reconnaissance, which included taking aerial photographs.

The internal combustion engine also brought about the development
of the airship. This came in two basic types: the non-rigid, popularly
known as the blimp; and the rigid form, of which the most well known
was the German Zeppelin, which had a metal frame. Both had
gondolas for the crew underneath and the Zeppelin had a small
gondola that could be lowered through the clouds to help navigation.
Long-range reconnaissance, especially maritime, was the airship's
main role in 1914.

The aircraft that went to war in 1914 were of three basic types:
monoplane and biplane tractor aircraft, with the engine in the nose; and
biplane pushers, with the engine mounted in the rear. They were used
by the armies on both the Eastern and Western Fronts from the outset

for reconnaissance. Von Hindenburg stated that air reconnaissance played a vital part in his victory over the Russians at Tannenberg. These scouts, as they were called, were unarmed, but their crews soon realised the importance of preventing opposing scouts from carrying out their mission. They therefore began to arm themselves with rifles, small bombs, and even metal darts.

Now commenced the evolution and development of the fighting scout. Machine-guns began to be mounted, but with tractor types there was a problem in that fire had to be directed outside the path beaten by the propeller blades. Hence a forward-firing gun had to be mounted on the upper wing, which made reloading difficult, or on the side of the cockpit, making accurate fire almost impossible. Pusher aircraft did not face this dilemma, but were generally less manoeuvrable than the single-seat tractor.

One way of overcoming the problem was to fit steel deflectors on the blades to enable the machine gun to fire through them. First to do this was the Frenchman Roland Garros with his Morane-Saulnier monoplane in spring 1915. The Dutch aircraft designer Anthony Fokker, who was developing aircraft for the Germans, perfected a concept that had already been examined, the interrupter gear, which enabled the machine gun's fire to be synchronised with the propeller. From August 1915 the German Fokkers dominated the skies. So dominant did they become that in early 1916 the British Royal Flying Corps laid down that every reconnaissance mission had to have armed escorts, and it was this which brought about the beginning of formation flying.

Reconnaissance itself remained just as important during the static conditions of trench warfare. Air photography, too, was perfected, and it was solely from this that accurate maps of the battle area were produced. In spring 1915 the deployment of aircraft to direct guns onto targets also became more effective with the development of air-to-ground radio.

Both sides on the Western Front also began to use tethered observation balloons in order to locate targets behind the trenches. These balloons not only became part of the scenery, but also a target in themselves for the fighting scout. Significantly, the men who manned these balloons were given parachutes, but they were not issued to aircraft crews until the Germans began to use them in 1918. The official British reason for this was that it might encourage pilots to leave their aircraft unnecessarily.

The Fokker scourge, as it was called on the Western Front, lasted for nine months before the British and French regained air supremacy. The main reason was that new Allied types, especially the British FE2b, a pusher, and the French Nieuport *Bebe*, had a superior performance to the monoplane Fokker Eindecker. They arrived in time for the Allies to enjoy air supremacy at the beginning of the Battle of the Somme in July 1916, but once again the tide soon turned.

Fokker, Albatros and Halberstadt quickly produced aircraft with a much better performance than the Allied types. The Germans also began to operate in the air in complete squadrons of 14 aircraft so that they would have numerical superiority over their opponents. The climax of this period of German air ascendancy over the Western Front came in April 1917. By this time, the Germans were sending up three or four squadrons together. These became known as circuses and the most famous was that led by Baron Manfred von Richthofen, called the Red Baron by the British on account of the all-red Albatros triplane he flew. The British, who alone lost some 150 aircraft destroyed and 316 aircrew killed or captured during the month, called it Bloody April.

Once more, though, the tide began to turn as the Allies also introduced new aircraft types. The French now had the Spad and the Nieuport 17, some of which the British also used. They themselves had already received the Sopwith Pup at the end of 1916. This was joined by the Sopwith triplane in spring 1917, considered by von Richthofen to be the outstanding Allied fighter, which would prompt Fokker to introduce a German triplane. There was also the versatile two-seater Bristol Fighter, affectionately known as the Brisfit, and the SE-5. It was not speed, however, which gave these aircraft the edge (during the four years of war, speeds rose no more than 40 miles per

hour from the 80 or 90 miles per hour achievable in 1914). Rather it was manoeuvrability.

While the main object of the battle for air supremacy was maintaining air reconnaissance, the fighting scout was taking on other roles. A new breed of combat aircraft, the day bomber, had come into being. The task of types like the British DH4 and DH9, the German AEG, and the French Breguet, was to attack targets like ammunition dumps, headquarters, and communications centres behind the immediate battle area, a role that later was to become known as interdiction. These bombers needed escorts and this gave the fighting scout another task.

There are certain instances whereby pilots would arrive in the morning as replacements and be dead by the afternoon and hadn't even unpacked their kit.

BRAD KING:
IMPERIAL WAR MUSEUM

From the beginning of the war there had been incidents of scouts dropping bombs on ground troops, and later attacking them with machine-gun fire, but it was not until mid-1917 that they began to be used formally as fighter-bombers during attacks across trenches. Not only could they help to destroy machine-gun nests and other points of resistance that were holding up the attackers, but they also provided valuable information on the progress of the attack. Ground strafing, as the pilots called it, demanded nerves of steel, since operating at very low level made them targets for every rifle and machine gun in the vicinity. Best known of the aircraft types that were used in this role was the Sopwith Camel, which first appeared in France in summer 1917. Not until the last few months of the war, however, was any thought given to providing the pilot with any protection against ground fire. The result was the Sopwith Salamander, which had slabs of armour plate around and under the cockpit.

By September 1918 air support for ground operations had been so perfected that General Billy Mitchell, commanding the American Air Service in France, could call on the services of no less than 1500 aircraft – French and American of all types – for the US attack at St Mihiel. Two-thirds, including heavy bombers, were employed on interdiction deep in the German rear, while the remainder undertook ground strafing missions.

The threat to the aircraft from the ground was not just from machine-gun and rifle fire. By the beginning of 1915 both sides had dedicated anti-aircraft guns, some static, but others mounted on trucks. It took time to grapple with the technicalities of achieving accurate fire against aircraft, but the pilots of both sides soon came to respect it.

. . . when it got above and behind our middle machine it dived on to it like a huge hawk on a hapless sparrow.

FLIGHT SERGEANT JAMES MCCUDDEN VC,
MEMOIR

(ABOVE) British radio-telegraph operators in the field. By the last months of the war, collaboration between ground forces and air support had been developed to such an extent that fighter-bombers could be called in to attack specific enemy targets which were holding up an advance.

The pattern of air warfare over the Western Front was mirrored in other theatres of war. Russian grappled with Austrian and German over the Eastern Front. In Salonika and on the Italian front, air fighting took place and, at times, reached almost the intensity of that in the skies of France and Flanders. In the Middle East, too, British aircraft fought German in Mesopotamia and Palestine. It was during the final September 1918 British offensive in Palestine that there was a stark demonstration of how airpower could affect land warfare. Retreating Turkish forces were trapped and then mercilessly pounded by bombs and machine-gun fire from the air.

Nowhere, though, was the air war more concentrated than on the Western Front, and it remained intense right up to the very end. On 10 November 1918, the day before the Armistice, there was a fierce fight between a patrol of Brisfits and a squadron of Fokker D VIIs, which was attacking a formation of DH9 day bombers.

The attraction of aircraft to navies was that they enabled them to see what was going on below the horizon. Initially, though, the problem was that maritime reconnaissance entailed

land-based aircraft with limited range, which was of no use to fleets on the high seas. The aeroplane had therefore to be able to operate from the ships themselves. The question was how? Two solutions suggested themselves.

The first was an exploit by a professional American pilot, Eugene Ely, who in November 1910 successfully flew his Curtiss pusher biplane off a specially constructed platform on the US cruiser *Birmingham*. Two months later he made a safe landing on another platform, this time aboard the USS *Pennsylvania*. This can be said to have marked the beginning of the concept of the aircraft carrier, but it was not immediately pursued.

Instead, navies preferred the idea of the floatplane which could land and take off from water. It was the Royal Navy which took the lead in this, converting an old light cruiser so that it could operate two floatplanes. These were lowered into the water to take off and then winched back in on landing. A further three such ships, all of them former cross-Channel steamers, were similarly converted at the beginning of the war. These were later joined by the former Cunarder *Campania* specifically for operations with the Grand Fleet. Not only could she carry up to 11 aircraft, but detachable trolleys were fitted to the floats of the seaplanes to enable them to make deck take-offs, although they still had to land on the water.

For long-range maritime reconnaissance, however, the airship was ideal, and at the start of the war this was the main role of the German Zeppelin. One of the first tasks of the Royal Naval Air Service was to reduce this threat. Three of their squadrons were deployed to Dunkirk and from here made bombing attacks on the Zeppelin bases at Düsseldorf and Cologne, with one Zeppelin being destroyed at the latter. Other attacks were also made from the three smaller seaplane tenders against Zeppelin construction works.

Apart from having observation balloons, capital ships also began to be equipped with a single seaplane in order to increase the fleet's reconnaissance capability. A significant development came with the mounting of a torpedo on the Short seaplane in order to give it an attack capability against ships. The first success of this new weapon came in August 1915 when it sank a Turkish steamer in the Sea of Marmara in the Dardanelles.

Airpower also began to be deployed against the submarine at an early stage in the war. The first efforts were made by the Royal Naval Air Service when its aircraft attacked a suspected U-boat base at Antwerp with bombs. The seaplane, however, lacked the endurance to be effective in the anti-submarine role, and other means were needed. One answer to the problem was the flying boat as opposed to the seaplane. The pioneer of this aircraft type was the American designer Glenn Curtiss. In 1916 Wing Commander Porte, commanding the Royal Naval Air Service base at Felixstowe on England's east coast, took Curtiss's H-12 Large America flying boat and adapted it for anti-submarine warfare. He strengthened its hull, armed it with seven machine-guns and two 230-lb bombs, and gave it an endurance of six hours' flying time. Its first success came in May 1917 when it sank a U-boat with a bomb.

The other solution was the non-rigid airship. Here the Admiralty produced the SS or submarine-searching airship, with a gondola made from the fuselage of the BE2C aircraft. By the end of the war these could remain aloft for 48 hours and were equipped with radio and bombs. While they certainly deterred U-boats, both in the North Sea and the Mediterranean, they did have their limitations. They were too unstable a platform to be accurate in bombing a pinpoint target like a U-boat and their operations were limited by the weather.

Work on developing a true aircraft carrier continued. One major step forward came in 1916 with the introduction of the Sopwith Pup, which had been ordered by the Royal Naval Air Service. This compact and highly manoeuvrable little fighter had an added advantage for the Royal Navy in that it had a very short take-off capability and could thus use the flight deck of the large seaplane carriers. However, the Pup still had to land in the water, from where, kept afloat by air bags, it was winched on board. The next stage was to launch it from a warship, flying off a platform built on one of the gun turrets, although the ship needed to steam into the wind for the aircraft to get airborne. Even so the British Grand Fleet now had a means of tackling the Zeppelins that continually shadowed it. The first success came in August 1917 when a Pup took off from the cruiser HMS *Yarmouth*, escorting minelayers off the Dutch coast, and reduced Zeppelin LZ23 to a mass of flames.

In that same month, August 1917, a Sopwith Pup was successfully landed on HMS *Furious*, the Royal Navy's first aircraft, as opposed to seaplane, carrier. It took much skill because the ship's bridge and funnels were amidships. Five days later the pilot, Flight Commander Dunning, was killed attempting the same manoeuvre, but his death was not in vain. *Furious* was redesigned to provide both a landing deck as well as a flying-off deck. The first aircraft carrier, as we now know it, had come into being.

Thus, by the end of the Great War, maritime airpower, although not yet playing a decisive role, had shown its potential influence on the war at sea. The ideas were there, but technology, aeronautical and nautical, needed to be further advanced before theory could effectively be demonstrated in practice.

The war of 1914–18 also witnessed airpower being used in another role. On 30 August 1914 a German Rumpler Taube two-seater reconnaissance aircraft dropped five small bombs on Paris, killing a woman and injuring two other people. In January 1915 the Kaiser sanctioned raids by Zeppelins against British naval and military installations. That same month the first such attack, by two Zeppelins, took place and killed four and injured 16 civilians on England's

We said, 'Look there it is!' A long black cigar-like shaped object coming very slowly. I put my arms around my mother and I can tell you I don't know how we felt.

CHRISTINE SMITH,
LETTER TO HER BROTHER

east coast. This was not intentional. The Zeppelins did not appear again until April. By then they were operating from Belgium, while others attacked targets in Poland in support of the German spring offensive against the Russians.

On the last night of May 1915 the first bombs were dropped on London and seven civilians were killed. By this time crude defences had been organised – a few guns and searchlights, and the dimming of street lights – but they were of little use. Nevertheless, a week later the

first victory of an aircraft over a Zeppelin occurred when a Royal Naval Air Service Morane-Saulnier Parasol on a bombing mission intercepted LZ37 over Bruges in Belgium. The Morane-Saulnier Parasol climbed above the Zeppelin and dropped its bombs on it.

During 1916 there was a renewed Zeppelin offensive against England, but the anti-Zeppelin defences improved, with squadrons of aircraft trained to operate by night being based around London. These accounted for five Zeppelins during the autumn, with a further two falling to anti-aircraft guns. Thereafter, only another 11 airship raids were undertaken because of their now clear vulnerability to improved aircraft types.

Improvements in aircraft range and payload had by now led to the development of the long-range bomber. Here it was the Italians and Russians who led the way. The former developed the Caproni Ca30 series during 1915–16, and these were soon winging their way over the Alps to attack targets in Austria, especially the port of Pola at the head of the Adriatic. The Russians, on the other hand, already had a large bomber in 1914, the four-engined Ilya Mourometz designed by Igor Sikorsky, later the helicopter pioneer. The Tsar's Squadron of Flying Ships, which operated them, flew some four hundred missions during 1914–17 with much success. Armed with several machine-guns, and

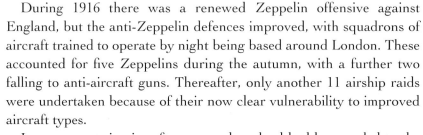

equipped with self-sealing fuel tanks, they were more than a match for fighters, with only one being lost to them.

On the Western Front during 1915 the French made a few scattered attacks on German towns in retaliation for occasional Zeppelin attacks on France, but it was not until spring 1917 that a concerted strategic bombing offensive got under way. The Germans had been developing long-range bombers and in May 1917 Gotha IV aircraft began to attack England by day from bases in Belgium. In mid-June London came under attack and civilian casualties were heavy, with well over 200 killed in two raids alone. There was a near-riot in the East End, and munition workers failed to turn up at their factories. Two crack fighter squadrons were hastily brought back from France and a committee was set up under the South African General Jan Smuts to make recommendations on how to overcome this menace. He recommended the installation of a system of defences around London consisting of anti-aircraft guns, aircraft, and early-warning systems. This was hastily put into effect, and did force the Germans, as had happened with their Zeppelins, to resort to attacks by night, bringing in giant Staaken bombers. By the following spring, however, the defences were proving effective and the last raid on London, in May 1918, resulted in six bombers being shot down. Even so, an American airman taking shelter in an Underground station during this raid noted that: 'It doesn't matter whether they hit anything or not as long as they put the wind up the civilian population so thoroughly. These people wanted peace and they wanted it badly.'

The desire to retaliate for the raids on London during the summer of 1917 was strong, and that autumn British bombers were sent to eastern France to begin attacks on targets in Germany. These included the giant Handley Page bomber, which had been developed for the Royal Naval Air Service for attacks on Zeppelin bases. Industrial targets in south-west Germany were selected, but the weather prevented more than a few raids during the winter.

General Smuts, in his report on the summer 1917 raids on London, had been struck by their profound effect on civilian morale and believed that the long-range bomber could play a decisive and important role by striking at the heart of the enemy's homeland, at the seat of government, industry, and the very will to wage war. This would give air forces a role totally independent of armies and navies, and hence they should be regarded as a separate armed service. The force of this argument impressed the British Government and the result was that on 1 April

1918 the Royal Flying Corps and Royal Naval Air Service were merged into the Royal Air Force.

But while the RAF continued to provide support for the Royal Navy and the Army, the growing force of strategic bombers in France was given the official title of the Independent Force to stress its separateness from the two older armed services. Throughout 1918, and in conjunction with French bombers, the Independent Force continued its operations against south-western Germany. The primitive bombsights of the time meant that inevitably civilians suffered, but the Force remained too small to have any significant effect. Indeed, it was calculated that the 675 strategic bombing raids carried out by the British and French during the war cost the lives of a mere 746 German soldiers and civilians and caused just £1.2 million worth of physical damage. The Germans, too, developed effective air defences and the Independent Force suffered, losing 72 machines in the last two and a half months of the war alone. There was, nonetheless, evidence that the effect on civilian morale as a result of bombing by both sides had been significant. General Hugh Trenchard, who commanded the RAF's Independent Force, commented in his Official Dispatch at the end of the war: 'The moral effect of bombing stands undoubtedly to the material effect in a proportion of twenty to one.'

When we were flying at about 17,000 feet
it gave you a wonderful feeling of exhilaration.
You were sort of 'I'm King of the Castle!'
You were up there and you were right out of the war.
I'd been in the infantry and we were always
lousy, filthy, dirty and very often hungry,
whereas in the Flying Corps it's a gentleman's life.

LIEUTENANT PERCY DOUGLAS:
11TH SQUADRON

(ABOVE) A French 'balloonautic', as the British troops called the crew of observation balloons, prepares to go aloft. Unlike aircraft crew of the time he is equipped with a parachute since the unwieldy balloons soon became a prime target for attack by enemy scouts, and the crews often had to make a quick escape.

As with maritime airpower during 1914–18, the experience of the combatant nations in strategic bombing, limited as it was, did appear to point the way to a new method of waging war. Given the long and bloody deadlock created by trench warfare, it seemed to some that airpower, acting on its own, could achieve quick and decisive victory at less cost than more traditional methods. It meant, however, that the civilian was now being placed ever more firmly in the firing line. Future war was thus likely to become increasingly total.

THE WORLD'S FIRST HEAVIER-THAN-AIR FLIGHT HAD TAKEN PLACE ONLY 11 YEARS EARLIER, BUT AIRCRAFT HAD AN IMMEDIATE EFFECT ON THE WAR.

(ABOVE) A German Aviatik C1 reconnaissance aircraft on the Eastern Front in 1914. Both sides were convinced that artillery observation was the main role for aircraft. As war began, the British and French had a combined strength of about 185 aircraft and the Germans about the same.

(TOP RIGHT) A machine-gun mounted in the nose of a British FE2B. The need to drive away enemy reconnaissance aircraft soon led to pilots using pistols and then machine-guns. The difficulty of firing through the propeller led to the development of several 'pusher' designs like this.

(BOTTOM RIGHT) A French Spad VII with synchronised forward firing machine-guns. Once the Dutchman Anthony Fokker had invented an interrupter mechanism which allowed machine-guns to be fired through the propeller, the development of the 'fighting scout' was rapid.

THE TECHNOLOGICAL RACE TO DEVELOP AND GET
INTO PRODUCTION EVER MORE AGILE, SWIFT AND
HEAVILY ARMED FIGHTERS DROVE AERIAL
WARFARE FORWARD AT AMAZING SPEED.

(TOP LEFT) A squadron of
French Nieuports prepares for
takeoff. The Nieuport *Bebe* was
the first Allied aircraft that
could take on the Fokker EIII
monoplane, which dominated
the winter of 1915–16.

(BOTTOM LEFT AND ABOVE)
The British SE-5 was the first
of a new breed of bigger
stronger fighters that allowed
the Allies to win back air
superiority from the German
Albatros scouts in the summer
of 1917.

THE NEW MACHINES BROUGHT A RAPID ADVANCE
BOTH IN ORGANISATION AND TACTICS.

(ABOVE) A British SE-5 gets into the perfect line astern position for an attack. Most pilots tried to get above their enemy and then dive in out of the sun. Once the enemy was on your tail only an immediate and steep diving turn could save your life.

(RIGHT) A single scout takes off on dawn patrol. Groups of fighters were soon being sent to escort vulnerable reconnaissance aircraft, and the Germans responded by attacking en masse, leading to dogfights which sometimes involved scores of aircraft.

We got into a dogfight this morning with a new brand of Fokkers . . . . This fellow just hung right there and sprayed me with lead like a hose.

LIEUTENANT JOHN GIRDER:
AMERICAN PILOT ATTACHED TO THE RFC

They were basically normal young men who might be killed any day and they lived life to the full. A lot of them did suffer very badly from nerves as time went on and they could see their death approaching.

PETER HART, HISTORIAN:
INTERVIEWED FOR THE PROGRAMME

FOR YOUNG MEN ON BOTH SIDES THE
OPPORTUNITY TO FLY SEEMED IRRESISTIBLE.
HOWEVER, THE REALITY OF AIR WARFARE
BECAME INCREASINGLY HORRIFIC.

(LEFT) French pilots posing. It was noticeable how quickly these young men, usually in their late teens or early twenties, ceased to look lighthearted as the reality of constant combat and the likelihood of death took its toll.

(ABOVE) Young pilots of the Royal Flying Corps setting off on a mission. By 1917 the life expectancy of a young pilot was 11 days from reaching his squadron. A great gulf soon separated the novice from the men who had experience.

A FEW PILOTS HAD THE SKILL, NERVE AND LUCK TO SURVIVE LONG ENOUGH
TO BECOME ACES. BUT FEW OF THEM COULD HOPE TO LAST INDEFINITELY.

(TOP LEFT) Germany's Baron Manfred von Richthofen, centre, arguably the most famous of all the World War I aces. He was shot down, possibly by ground fire, in June 1918, having claimed a total of 80 kills.

(BOTTOM LEFT) The frail figure of French ace Georges Guynemer showing off his favourite Spad. Leader of the elite French squadron 'The Storks', he scored 45 kills, but by the end was unable to sleep and moved as if in a trance.

(ABOVE) The Red Baron pulling on his flying suit beside his famous all red Fokker Triplane with which he led the crack Jagdstaffel 11. Ruthless, cold-blooded and a crack shot, he once said: 'When I have shot down an Englishman my hunting passion is satisfied for quarter of an hour.'

SOME AMERICAN PILOTS HAD BECOME ACES EVEN
BEFORE THEIR COUNTRY BEGAN FIGHTING.

(ABOVE) Raoul Lufbery in the uniform of a US major. Although born French, he taught the Escadrille Lafayette – a squadron of US volunteers who flew for France before their country entered the war – and then transferred to the US Army air corps.

(TOP RIGHT) When Lufbery was killed, having made 17 kills, the US Army gave him a funeral worthy of royalty. (BOTTOM RIGHT) One of the few survivors, Eddie Rickenbacker of the 94th Aero Squadron, America's ace of aces with 26 kills.

PILOTS DID NOT HAVE PARACHUTES, AND THE
FEAR OF BEING SHOT DOWN IN FLAMES WAS
THEIR RECURRING NIGHTMARE.

(TOP LEFT) French troops and
a doctor and nurse gather
around a wounded pilot who
had managed to get his aircraft
down more or less intact. If
they did not catch fire, the
aeroplanes of the period could
glide for miles.

(BOTTOM LEFT) Fitters
salvaging what they can from a
badly damaged aircraft.

(ABOVE) A crashed American
aircraft. Almost as frightful as
catching fire, was being caught
in an uncontrollable spin.

SHOOTING DOWN OBSERVATION BALLOONS WAS
THE SCOUT PILOT'S LEAST FAVOURITE DUTY.

(ABOVE) Raising an American observation balloon. Hundreds of these were used by both sides all along the front throughout the war to direct artillery fire and spot enemy dispositions. Shooting them down was like putting the enemy's eyes out.

(TOP RIGHT) The observers in a British balloon. They used telephones to communicate with the ground, and had parachutes to escape from their sitting targets.

(BOTTOM RIGHT) Anti-aircraft gunners defending a balloon.

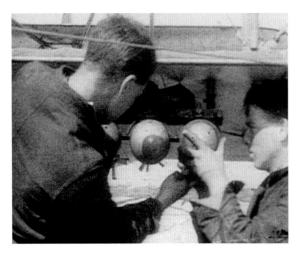

(TOP) Radio telegraph operators in action. Once reconnaissance aircraft and observation balloons had reported enemy positions, new types of aircraft were developed to attack them.

(MIDDLE) At first it was various types of scout or reconnaissance aircraft like this British FE2B that were adapted for bombing and ground attack. Sometimes, in the early days, the observer would simply throw the bombs over the side.

(BOTTOM) British aircrew mounting light bombs on a FE2B. By 1917 proper bomb racks had been developed, and crews were learning how to allow for set-off when dropping their bombs. But it was still a somewhat hit-and-miss affair.

(ABOVE RIGHT) A squadron of Sopwith Salamander ground-attack aircraft starts up in the autumn of 1918. This was one of the first specialised ground-attack aircraft and its pilot's cockpit was armoured for protection. By the last year of the war close air support of ground forces had become an important part of warfare.

THE FIRST EXPERIMENTS AT DROPPING BOMBS FROM AIRCRAFT HAD BEGUN
BEFORE THE WAR, AND TECHNIQUES DEVELOPED SWIFTLY.

*Many went out with as little as five hours
training. The two lads I crossed the channel
with . . . were both shot down before I had
been over the lines.*

HAROLD SEYMOUR:
ROYAL FLYING CORPS

BY THE END OF THE WAR, LONG-RANGE BOMBERS
HAD BROUGHT CIVILIANS INTO THE FRONT LINE
FOR THE FIRST TIME.

(ABOVE) A line-up of British Handley Page 0/400 heavy bombers. Capable of carrying 2000 lb of bombs over a range of 650 miles at 97 miles an hour, they had been specially designed to attack enemy industry and communications far behind the lines. A new form of warfare had been born.

(TOP AND BOTTOM RIGHT) The Germans were the first to use strategic bombing when they attacked London, in 1915 with Zeppelin airships and then in 1917 with long-range Gotha bombers. The British were the first to develop anti-aircraft defences, combining early warning systems, guns, searchlights and fighters. A police car in 1917 with an air-raid warning notice.

(TOP LEFT) A British Type A non-rigid airship. The Royal Navy was quick to see how this sort of craft could immensely increase the range at which it could spot and attack the enemy. These craft carried a three-man crew with bombs or depth charges. They could stay aloft for up to 36 hours with a top speed of 45 miles an hour and a range of 1500 miles.

(BOTTOM LEFT) The Royal Navy found that with their range the airships were particularly suitable for anti-submarine work. World War I submarines had only a limited underwater range, and the constant threat of being spotted by an airship placed an extra constraint on their use.

THE NEED TO SEE OVER THE HORIZON SOON PERSUADED NAVIES THAT AIRCRAFT MUST GO TO SEA.

(ABOVE) Other British developments were flying boats like the Felixstowe F-2A (TOP) that were far quicker and more manoeuvrable than the airships, and seaplanes that accompanied the fleet on special carriers. But they were cumbersome, having to be winched on and off the ships, and were unable to take off in rough seas.

The first thing we had to do was to learn to fly on and off the foredeck. I remember the captain said, 'You may as well take a revolver and blow your brains out!'

WILLIAM HAWKINS: RNAS,
HMS *FURIOUS*

(LEFT) A Sopwith Pup of the Royal Naval Air Service takes off from a platform on the gun turret of a cruiser. The disadvantage was that once the fighter had completed the mission it had to ditch in the sea, and hopefully be winched back intact for another flight. This rarely happened without damage to the aircraft, let alone to the nerves of the pilot.

(ABOVE) A Pup attempts to land on a platform built at the stern of the British battleship *Furious*. It is fitted with skids which were meant to go under ropes on the deck and slow it down. Finally, in 1918, the British put a complete flight deck on HMS *Argus* so that aircraft could both land on and take off what was the world's first true aircraft carrier.

THIS SEA WAR WAS ABOUT INNOVATION AND DAZZLING ADVANCES IN TECHNOLOGY

4 BATTLE FLEETS AND U-BOATS
Naval Warfare 1914–1918

There is great enthusiasm in the British Isles due to the war and recruits are flocking in daily. If only the German Fleet would come out we would wipe them out in a few minutes.

LIEUTENANT ERIC WOODRUFF

In time of war, opposing navies strive to obtain freedom of action in the seas and oceans and to cut off each other's maritime communications. Traditionally this has best been done by bringing the enemy's fleet to battle and destroying it. The navies of the two sides went to war in 1914 with this very much in mind.

The main tool of their trade was the battleship, which had undergone a major change in the decade before 1914, with the introduction of the dreadnought (see Chapter 1).

The original HMS *Dreadnought* had ten 12-inch guns, but by 1914 she had been totally eclipsed by HMS *Queen Elizabeth* with her eight 15-inch guns. Supporting the battleships were cruisers, which had two roles. They were the fleet's scouts, but also had to protect the battleships from attack by torpedo boat destroyers, the third element of the fleet. The dreadnought had, besides firepower, considerably higher speed than the old-style battleship, so much so that it outstripped the existing cruisers, as well as outgunning them. In 1908, therefore, the British launched HMS *Invincible*, a battle-cruiser: fast and with guns only slightly less powerful than the dreadnought. In order to achieve high speeds, some armoured protection was sacrificed, but not on the German versions, which were also known as armoured cruisers. It was

a sacrifice that the British would later have cause to regret. But battle-cruisers were expensive to build and for Britain, whose navy ranged over every ocean, there was a particular need for a vessel that would dominate the more remote seas. Consequently, the light cruiser was developed in tandem with the battle-cruiser.

The torpedo was developed during the second half of the nineteenth century and, in order to protect capital ships from this threat, the torpedo boat destroyer was introduced. This became the third main element of the battle fleet and soon took on other roles as well, including reconnaissance and as a torpedo launcher in its own right. Another method of launching a torpedo was by submarine, but more on this later.

The other threat to ships besides guns and torpedoes was the mine. Mines could be laid by submarine or surface ship, but during the war specialised minelayers were developed. Likewise, in order to clear mines, minesweepers came into service.

At the outbreak of war in 1914 the opposing fleets deployed to their wartime bases. The Royal Navy, still very much the world's largest, had the Grand Fleet at Scapa Flow in the Orkney Islands, and the Mediterranean Fleet based at Malta. It also had squadrons in the West Indies and South Atlantic, and could call on the small New Zealand and Australian navies. The French agreed with the British to concentrate on the Mediterranean, using their base at Toulon. The German High Seas Fleet was based at Kiel and Wilhelmshafen. In the Mediterranean, the Austro-Hungarian navy operated from the head of the Adriatic, but its ships had to pass through the narrow Straits of Otranto, which were easy to blockade. The same situation applied in the Black Sea, where exit into the Mediterranean could only be effected via the Dardanelles, and once at sea the Russian ships based at Sevastopol and Odessa faced the Turks from Constantinople and Trebizond. Russia, too, had another fleet in the Baltic, but its activities were severely restricted by the German presence there.

The British plan was to contain the German High Seas Fleet in the North Sea by denying it access through the Straits of Dover and using the Grand Fleet to patrol from the Orkneys to the Norwegian coast. They hoped that the Germans would quickly come out of port to do battle, but this was not to be. The German aim, on the other hand, was to destroy the Grand Fleet by attacking one element at a time. They were also determined to restrict British shipping movements by mining coastal waters.

Besides trying to restrict the movement of British shipping through mining, the Germans also used the U-boat (*Unterseeboot* – submarine) to locate the Grand Fleet, while the British sent submarines into the Baltic. There were a number of minor clashes in the North Sea, which culminated in a British destroyer and light cruiser raid on Heligoland at the end of

> *Jellicoe's main fear was that if he took his very expensive battle fleet to sea and he lost a battle, he effectively as he put it might lose the war in an afternoon.*
>
> CAPTAIN RICHARD WOODMAN, Naval Historian:
> INTERVIEWED FOR THE PROGRAMME

August. In this the Germans lost three light cruisers and a destroyer was sunk.

At the outbreak of war the Germans had a number of warships at sea. Two of these were the cruisers *Goeben* and *Breslau*. They had originally been given orders to bombard Algiers in order to interrupt the passage of French colonial troops to France. They were then ordered to sail for Turkey, but their commander nonetheless bombarded Algiers early on 4 August, then set off to run the gauntlet of the British and French fleets. The two ships arrived at Constantinople on 10 August. Now they began a campaign of bombarding the Russian coast and harrying shipping in the Black Sea.

A more significant overseas German naval force was the Far East Squadron under Admiral Graf von Spee. One of its ships, the light cruiser *Emden*, caused havoc in the Indian Ocean before being surprised and sunk by the Australian cruiser *Sydney* in the Cocos Islands.

The remainder of the Far East Squadron had orders to harry Allied trade in the Pacific. Setting off from the German-owned Caroline Islands, von Spee steamed with two battle-cruisers and a light cruiser towards South America, causing chaos on the trade routes. A British squadron based on the Falkland Islands was ordered to hunt down von Spee, who had now been joined by two further light cruisers. The two forces clashed on 1 November 1914 off Coronel on the Chilean coast. The British, whose ships were largely obsolete, suffered badly, losing two of their four ships. Two modern battle-cruisers were hastily sent out from Britain and revenge was gained off the Falkland Islands on 8 December. Four out of the five German ships were sunk, with the one survivor, the light cruiser *Dresden*, being hunted down and destroyed in March 1915. This marked the end of German naval activity outside home waters, apart from that by U-boats.

In January 1915, there was a serious clash in the North Sea off the Dogger Bank. Intercepting German radio signals indicating that their battle-cruisers were making a foray,

Admiral David Beatty and his 1st Battle Squadron of five battle-cruisers intercepted and engaged four German ships. Beatty's flagship, HMS *Lion*, was hit several times and badly damaged, but the *Seydlitz* had two turrets destroyed. Worse, the *Bluecher* was sunk. The loss of the *Bluecher* caused the Germans to switch to submarine warfare, while British attention turned elsewhere.

The plan to send an expedition to the Dardanelles was spearheaded by the Royal Navy, especially Winston Churchill, its ministerial head as First Lord of the Admiralty. His original scheme was to force the Narrows into the Black Sea and destroy the *Goeben* and

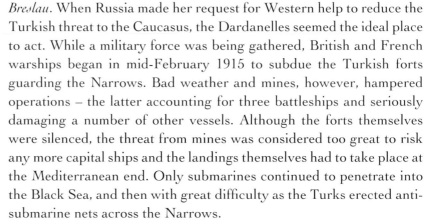

Breslau. When Russia made her request for Western help to reduce the Turkish threat to the Caucasus, the Dardanelles seemed the ideal place to act. While a military force was being gathered, British and French warships began in mid-February 1915 to subdue the Turkish forts guarding the Narrows. Bad weather and mines, however, hampered operations – the latter accounting for three battleships and seriously damaging a number of other vessels. Although the forts themselves were silenced, the threat from mines was considered too great to risk any more capital ships and the landings themselves had to take place at the Mediterranean end. Only submarines continued to penetrate into the Black Sea, and then with great difficulty as the Turks erected anti-submarine nets across the Narrows.

Elsewhere in the Mediterranean, the Italian entry into the war in May 1915 helped to keep the Austro-Hungarian fleet largely bottled up in its port of Pola in the northern Adriatic but, even so, single Austrian ships did occasionally manage to break out. German U-boats also began to use Pola as a base. In early 1916 the Allies constructed a barrage across the Otranto Straits, but U-boats and Austrian warships were still able to penetrate it and did so well into 1918.

In January 1916, Admiral Reinhard von Scheer, took over the German High Seas Fleet. He resumed raids on the English east coast and then, after the Germans had called off their unrestricted U-boat campaign in early May for fear of provoking American entry into the war, drew up a plan designed to trap and destroy elements of the British Grand Fleet. Battle-cruisers sailing off the Norwegian coast were to tempt Admiral Beatty's battle-cruisers out from their base at Rosyth in Scotland. The German dreadnoughts would then destroy them before the main body of the Grand Fleet under Sir John Jellicoe could arrive from Scapa Flow. The date chosen was 31 May.

Sensing from an intercepted radio signal that the Germans were up to something, Jellicoe decided to pre-empt them by putting to sea, ordering Beatty to rendezvous with him on the afternoon of the 31st off the entrance to the Skagerrak, which separates Danish Jutland from Norway. The Germans themselves sailed in the early hours of the 31st, with Admiral Hipper's battle-cruisers 50 miles ahead of the main body.

Beatty arrived at the rendezvous first and then clashed with Hipper. It soon became clear that the German gunnery was superior, largely thanks to their stereoscopic rangefinders. Four out of six of Beatty's battle-cruisers were badly hit, with three blown up. Beatty's supporting battleships now arrived and began to pound Hipper, whose ships continued to give as good as they got, sinking another battle-cruiser.

The German main body now appeared, and Beatty withdrew northward towards Jellicoe. Von Scheer, who had only 16 battleships compared with 24 British, followed Beatty, unaware that Jellicoe was now approaching. It was 6.30 p.m. and Jellicoe, now conscious of von Scheer's presence, altered course in an attempt to cut him off from his base. The main battle fleets began to pound one another, but while the German gunnery remained superior, the weight of British fire soon began to tell. Recognising the threat that Jellicoe posed, von Scheer made a 180-degree turn, which put him on a heading for home. He then turned east again, probably hoping to slip through the Skagerrak behind the British fleet, which was steaming on a parallel course. Von Scheer had miscalculated the Grand Fleet's speed, however, and found himself heading directly for it. The British ships renewed their fire and, in desperation, von Scheer sent in his destroyers. This caused Jellicoe to shy away, enabling von Scheer to make a second 180-degree turn before slipping away into the growing darkness. Jellicoe followed him, engaging at long range, but the twilight made it increasingly difficult to gauge the fall of shot, although he did sink two light cruisers at the cost of one of his own. Finally the British destroyers were sent in. They managed to sink the pre-dreadnought battleship *Pommern*, and another German ship was lost to a British-laid minefield, but, otherwise, von Scheer was able to make good his escape.

In August 1916 von Scheer made another foray into the North Sea and was very nearly trapped by the Grand Fleet in the same way, although no shots were fired. After this the High Seas Fleet remained in port. Thus, Jellicoe, while bested at a tactical level at Jutland, did eventually achieve a strategic victory after a fashion in that the German fleet was dissuaded from putting to sea again. Instead, the Germans turned once more to the U-boat, a weapon that had already displayed potential to affect the course of the war.

Navies saw the roles of the submarine as the sinking of opposing warships, reconnaissance and minelaying. Very soon, however, the submarine was to prove itself more of a threat to merchant shipping than to warships.

The dominance of British seapower in 1914 meant that it took only a few weeks to bring German merchant shipping to a halt, except in the Baltic. The Germans therefore had to rely on neutral shipping, and pre-war international agreements laid down that only certain types of goods could be declared contraband and that a neutral ship had to be bound for an enemy port for its cargo to be seized. The British answer to this was to purchase the cargo compulsorily, then allow the ship to return to its home port.

The Germans were in no position to blockade British trade, but what they could quite legitimately do was attack and sink Allied merchant vessels, provided the safety of their crews was ensured. A number of warships and armed merchant vessels were deployed for this very purpose, but most were quickly hunted down and destroyed.

This left the U-boat, but this had limitations. It could not easily escort a vessel into harbour and did not have the manpower to put a prize crew aboard. It also could not guarantee the safety of a captured crew because it had no room on board. The best it could do was to order the crew into their lifeboats and then sink the ship, preferably by gunfire in order to preserve torpedoes. From October 1914 this was the practice that the Germans began to adopt.

The U-boat captain was, however, putting his boat at risk when he surfaced and, even at the end of 1914, Germany only had 28 submarines. The admirals began to argue that the only way to counter the British blockade was to attack merchant vessels underwater without warning. The German government, and indeed the Kaiser himself, resisted this, but after the reverse suffered by the surface fleet at the Battle of Dogger Bank in January 1915 they relented.

The Lusitania *is a godsend to the British. It's quite the most stupid thing the Germans could have done.*

PROFESSOR ANDREW LAMBERT, KING'S COLLEGE LONDON:
INTERVIEWED FOR THE PROGRAMME

The following month the Germans declared a policy of unrestricted submarine warfare in the waters surrounding Britain and Ireland. While care would be taken not to sink neutral vessels, their safety could not be guaranteed.

The campaign made little immediate impact because of the limited number of U-boats. Furthermore, the use of anti-submarine nets and surface patrols began to take a toll of U-boats. In May 1915, however, an event took place which was to have serious implications for the policy. On the 1st the Cunard passenger liner *Lusitania* left New York for Liverpool. Six days later, off south-west Ireland, the ship was sunk by a single torpedo fired by U-20. Of the two thousand people aboard her, 1198 were drowned, including 128 Americans.

There was an immediate outcry over this atrocity, both in Britain and the United States. Yet the *Lusitania* was carrying contraband goods in the form of explosives and ammunition. But although there was a surge of anti-German feeling in America, the sinking fuelled the belief that the war was uncivilised and, to use President Wilson's words, America was 'too proud to fight'.

Thus, the campaign continued for the remainder of 1915, petering out simply because so few U-boats could be maintained at sea at any one time. Even though some 1.3 million gross tons of merchant shipping were lost – some 65 per cent of it British – it had little effect on commerce. On 24 March 1916, however, an English Channel steamer, the *Sussex*, was torpedoed with more American lives being lost. This provoked the American government into a much stiffer reaction. If the Germans did not cease this form of warfare, the United States would have no option but to sever diplomatic relations. Fearful that this might lead to the United States entering the war, the Germans halted the campaign and merchant shipping losses fell dramatically. Instead, they turned to the Mediterranean, where fewer American ships sailed.

Throughout the first unrestricted campaign the U-boats used did not carry more than eight torpedoes and had to employ them sparingly. Thus 80 per cent of the ships destroyed were sunk by gunfire. Taking note of this, in 1915 the British developed a new anti-submarine weapon, the Q-ship. This was a seemingly innocent merchant vessel which would purposely sail into a U-boat danger area. When a U-boat surfaced guns would suddenly be unmasked and aim a quick barrage at the U-boat.

In August 1916, with the decision to keep the High Seas Fleet in port and the British blockade of Germany becoming ever tighter, the policy

of unrestricted submarine warfare was re-examined. The rate of U-boat construction had been rapidly rising and this was reflected in a parallel rise in ship sinkings during the second half of 1916. It was argued that British commerce could be crippled sufficiently to force the country to sue for peace. One factor above all others, however, caused a delay in coming to a decision. Throughout 1916 President Wilson had been putting out feelers to both sides in the hope of being able to broker a peace. There was to be a presidential election in

November 1916 and much depended on its outcome and the new president's attitude to Germany's terms for peace. In fact, Wilson was re-elected, but not until the end of December did he make it clear that he did not accept Germany's peace proposals. Consequently, in early January 1917, the Germans resolved on a wholesale unrestricted submarine campaign, with neutral ships given no leeway.

At the beginning of this new campaign, which began on 1 February 1917, some 110 U-boats were in commission. The boats were of two types: ocean-going, operating from German North Sea ports; and shorter-range coastal boats, based in Belgian ports. But besides Q-ships, which were now losing their effectiveness, anti-submarine nets and surface ships, the British now had a number of new weapons. Hydrophones could detect a U-boat's engine under the surface, provided it was close to the ship. Radio direction-finding – obtaining bearings on a U-boat's radio signals – had also come into use. Depth charges had been developed, although production of them was slow. Conventional mines had been used against submarines since the beginning of the war, but British types were poorly designed, and not until summer 1917 would an effective mine, the H Type, come into service. A new type of specialist anti-submarine vessel, the shallow-draught sloop, was being increasingly employed. Airpower, too, was beginning to be used.

However, the U-boats still succeeded in sinking no less than 500 ships during February and March 1917, and sailings of neutral ships in the eastern Atlantic and North Sea fell by 75 per cent.

One reason for the German success was that the new types of U-boat carried twice as many torpedoes as their predecessors. Another, though, was the traditional Royal Navy strategy of attack. Offensive patrols were sent out to sweep the main sea routes, but the U-boats merely sat on the fringes, waited for the patrols to pass, and then pounced on their prey. If sinkings continued at this high rate it was clear that it would not be long before Britain began to starve. To ward this off, strict food rationing had to be instituted.

Two days after the opening of the campaign, President Wilson, as he had threatened almost a year earlier, severed diplomatic relations with Germany. Two months later, on 6 April 1917, he declared war. Now the US Navy could help in eradicating the U-boat menace, but ships, aircraft, and airships on their own were not enough. The concept of anti-submarine warfare had to be rethought urgently.

The main solution to overcoming the U-boat threat was the convoy. The Royal Navy had resisted using it for three reasons. Convoys took a long time to assemble and organise, they were too defensive, and would merely invite increased U-boat attack. The US Navy also expressed the same doubts. Now, at the end of April, with ever-mounting losses, they were forced to try convoying. The results were startling. Out of 800 ships convoyed during July and August 1917 only five were lost. The following month, the ten U-boats sunk exceeded German monthly submarine construction for the first time in the war.

The U-boat threat had been brought under control, although sinkings of merchant vessels would continue until almost the very end of the war. In contrast, the Allied blockade of the Central Powers had progressively become tighter and tighter. Within both Germany and Austro-Hungary war exhaustion and discontent were on the increase.

The all big gun battleship was in a sense the lineal descendant of Nelson's day. The idea of throwing a huge weight of metal over the greatest distance and destroying the enemy. . . . War had changed. All that glamour had gone. It was now about logistics, survival, protection of trade and defeating the enemy that way.

CAPTAIN RICHARD WOODMAN, NAVAL HISTORIAN:
INTERVIEWED FOR THE PROGRAMME

IN 1914 THE GREAT FLEETS OF BATTLESHIPS SEEMED TO DOMINATE THE SEAS. BUT THE WRITING WAS ON THE WALL.

(ABOVE) The massive 15-inch guns of HMS *Queen Elizabeth*. Completed just after the war began, she and her four sisterships outgunned every other battleship in the world. But the threat of the torpedo and the mine was already causing concern to far-sighted naval officers.

(TOP RIGHT) HMS *Dreadnought*, the first 'all big gun' battleship. Her main armament of ten 12-inch guns, compared with the usual four, and high speed made all others obsolete – unfortunately including all earlier British types. Her appearance added impetus to the naval race which had already begun between Britain and Germany.

The only issue . . . is the number of Dreadnoughts!
No matter who tries to fight the Dreadnought,
the Dreadnought gobbles them all up! It's the armadillo
and the ants – the armadillo puts out its tongue
and licks up the ants.

ADMIRAL LORD FISHER

Essentially, it is [the dreadnought] a quantum leap in the performance of a battleship.
For a period of eight years you have a sustained building race in which ever bigger and more powerful battleships are built in competition.

PROFESSOR ANDREW LAMBERT, KING'S COLLEGE LONDON:
INTERVIEWED FOR THE PROGRAMME

(Top left) A German *Nassau*-class dreadnought battleship enters the Kiel Canal in 1913. Laid down within six months of the appearance of HMS *Dreadnought*, these four ships gave Germany a real chance to catch up with the huge lead that Britian had in pre-dreadnought battleships. By 1914 Germany had 13 of these new ships, compared with Britain's 22.

(Above) Grand Admiral Alfred von Tirpitz who became head of Germany's navy in 1897. He believed that building up a powerful fleet was the only way in which Germany could become a world power. The threat that this posed to the Royal Navy was the principal reason why Britain sought an alliance with France and Russia.

(TOP RIGHT) U-boat lookouts scan the horizon. The submarines had an underwater endurance of only a few hours, and spent much of their time on the surface, attacking with guns rather than their few precious torpedoes whenever possible. Merchant ships tended to sail alone and unescorted, so they were easy meat if they could be found.

(BOTTOM RIGHT) The liner *Lusitania* leaving New York on her last voyage. The Germans had announced a zone of 'unrestricted submarine warfare' around the British isles in February 1915, in which all vessels – including neutrals might be attacked without warning. The sinking of the *Lusitania* in May with the loss of 1198 lives, including many Americans, was a propaganda disaster.

IT WAS A SMALL AND UNTRIED WEAPON
WHICH SOON UPSET ALL PREVIOUS
ASSUMPTIONS ABOUT THE WAR AT SEA.

(TOP) A British B-class submarine loading a torpedo. In 1914 the Royal Navy had 73, compared with Germany's 37, but the British tended to be far smaller.

(ABOVE) A German U-boat commander looking for his prey. The Germans tried to counter-blockade Britain but were hampered by the Rules of War which in 1914 demanded that ships' crews were allowed to take to the boats.

THE FIRST UNRESTRICTED U-BOAT CAMPAIGN
GAVE THE ROYAL NAVY A STARK WARNING THAT
NAVAL WARFARE HAD CHANGED.

(TOP LEFT) A U-boat crew
mans the 88-mm gun carried
by all ocean-going U-boats.

(BOTTOM LEFT) In March 1916
U-boat commanders were told
to go back to stopping vessels
before sinking them . Even
though the first unrestricted
campaign had not had a massive
effect on British shipping, it had
forced the Royal Navy to divert
ships to anti-submarine warfare.

(ABOVE) The British Grand
Fleet on exercise at sea. The
threat from U-boats and mines
meant that neither the British
nor the German High Seas
Fleet ventured far out from
port for the first two years of
the war. The great battle which
many had anticipated would
decide in one go the war at sea
was slow in coming.

WHEN THE GREAT FLEETS FINALLY CLASHED IT WAS AN ANTI-CLIMAX. THE BRITISH LOST MORE SHIPS IN BATTLE, BUT WON THE STRATEGIC WAR.

(TOP LEFT) Battleships of the British Grand Fleet. In May 1916 the Germans launched an operation to lure out the battle-cruisers of Admiral David Beatty (BOTTOM RIGHT) and destroy them before the main Grand Fleet under Sir John Jellicoe (BOTTOM LEFT) could come to their aid.

(ABOVE) The British battleship HMS *Barham* turning to starboard at speed. She was one of the *Queen Elizabeth*-class which proved its worth at Jutland unlike the lightly armoured battle-cruisers. Beatty lost three due to magazine explosions before Jellicoe's Grand Fleet arrived.

ON 1 FEBRUARY 1917
THE GERMANS BEGAN
A SECOND
UNRESTRICTED
U-BOAT CAMPAIGN.
THE RESULTS WERE
IMMEDIATELY
DRAMATIC.

(ABOVE) A sign near Ypres shows the urgency of the crisis as shipping losses soared in the spring of 1917. As early as February Lord Derby, the secretary of state for war, reported to Haig that he was being asked 'whether our armies can win the war before our navy loses it'.

(RIGHT) A starving old lady in Germany. By 1916 the British blockade of German ports was causing serious shortages. Germany's ability to continue the war was not threatened, but the knowledge of how badly their families were suffering did affect the morale of the army severely.

The British blockade means they can't import food. So very steadily the Germans find their rations being cut and from a diet rich in animal fats they end up living on turnips.

PROFESSOR ANDREW LAMBERT, King's College London:
INTERVIEWED FOR THE PROGRAMME

THE THREAT THAT THE U-BOATS WOULD STARVE BRITAIN INTO DEFEAT
BROUGHT A DESPERATE SEARCH FOR WAYS TO COMBAT THEM.

(TOP LEFT) A hydrophone
operator seeks his prey.
At first it could only be used
when an escort vessel was
stationary because of propeller
noise. However, by the
summer of 1917, a version
which could be towed behind a
moving ship had been
introduced.

(BOTTOM LEFT) A British
Acasta-class destroyer.
Weighing just over 1300 tons
and armed with three 4-inch
guns and two 21-inch
torpedoes, she is typical of the
escort vessels pressed into
service for anti-submarine
work and convoys.

(ABOVE) A British rating
stands by to fire a depth charge
from a projector. Usually they
were rolled over the stern. An
effective type had been
developed by mid-1916, but
it had to detonate close to a
U-boat's hull and there were
never enough of them.

EVEN AFTER THE INTRODUCTION OF CONVOYS, THE ROYAL NAVY BELIEVED
THAT THE BEST FORM OF DEFENCE AGAINST U-BOATS WAS ATTACK.

(TOP LEFT) A Felixstowe flying boat at its base on Britain's east coast. Introduced in 1917, this had a top speed of 95 miles per hour and an endurance of six hours. Carrying four crew with up to seven machine-guns and 460-lbs of bombs, they proved an excellent anti-U-boat weapon.

(BOTTOM LEFT) A crew unleashes the concealed gun on a British Q-ship. These apparently unarmed merchant ships patrolled known U-boat routes, hoping that one would take the bait and surface for an attack. Once it did so, the guns would be revealed and the U-boat engaged.

(ABOVE) Navy reservists repairing the floats on netting of the 'Dover Barrage'. This barrier of steel mesh kept up by fishermen's floats was strung across the narrowest part of the English Channel so as to prevent U-boats slipping through into the Atlantic from their main base in Belgium.

By the end of the war, naval warfare had dramatically altered, more so than many naval officers were ready to accept.

(ABOVE) The 15-inch guns of the monitor HMS *Erebus*. She was used for shore bombardment and played an important role in the preparations for the special operations at Zeebrugge and Ostend when attempts were made to block the Belgian ports through which the U-boats emerged from their base at Bruges.

(TOP RIGHT) The crew of a British minesweeping trawler attempting to explode a mine with rifle fire.

(BOTTOM RIGHT) The Austro-Hungarian battleship *Svent Istvan* rolls over after being hit by Italian motor torpedo boats in the Adriatic on 10 June 1918. Her sinking showed the vulnerability of the capital ship to the new weapons.

THE WAR ON THE EASTERN FRONT WOULD RESHAPE THE MAP OF EUROPE FOREVER

5 WAR OF THE EAGLES

Eastern Front 1914–1918

. . . many could not even load their rifles and as for their shooting the less said about it the better. Such people could not really be considered soldiers at all.

GENERAL ALEXEI BRUSILOV: RUSSIAN CHIEF-OF-STAFF,
LETTER TO HIS WIFE, 1915

The war on the Eastern Front was a much more complex and mobile affair than that in the West. Not only did it involve the major powers of Germany, Austro-Hungary and Russia, but also the small nations of the turbulent Balkans and Turkey. The conflict therefore evolved into campaigns on a number of sub-fronts. The style of warfare also involved advances and retreats being measured in tens of miles rather than hundreds of feet.

As in the West, the initial war plans largely failed, as we have seen. In particular, Austro-Hungary was unable to deal Serbia an early knock-out blow. The Serbians eventually drove the Austrians back across the Danube by mid-December 1914.

The Russians, though they had suffered a quarter of a million casualties by mid-September 1914, were undeterred because their unwieldy mobilisation was only just getting into gear as their troop trains rolled westward. The Russian commander-in-chief, the Grand Duke Nicholas, uncle of Tsar Nicholas II, decided to strike at Silesia. The Germans were not confident that the Austrians would be able to deal with such an attack, so von Hindenburg and Ludendorff reduced their strength in East Prussia by two-thirds and sent these forces, as the German Ninth Army, to reinforce the Austrians.

The Germans then advanced through the southernmost region of Poland towards Warsaw, the main Russian supply base. Grand Duke Nicholas deployed his armies on the Vistula and, in order to strike the Germans in the flank, north of Warsaw. Crossing the Vistula on 9 October, the Germans closed on Warsaw but, with the Russian threat to their flank, they decided to withdraw. The Russians had also advanced into East Prussia once more, but did not press home their advance and soon came to a halt.

Further south, in the meantime, the Austrians had also attacked and succeeded in relieving the fortress of Przemysl. However, the Russian defences on the River San proved too strong for a further advance eastward. Then, as the Germans withdrew from outside Warsaw, the Russians attacked the Austrians, driving them back once more and again isolating Przemysl.

The Russians now resumed preparations for their thrust into Silesia, but, as before the battle of Tannenberg, poor radio security alerted the Germans. Von Mackensen's hard-marching Ninth Army was therefore hurriedly moved northward and struck the Russians at Lodz. Eventually the Russians withdrew towards Warsaw. Both sides now paused for breath.

While it was clear that the Germans were superior to the Russians, who were beginning to suffer from a serious shortage of artillery and ammunition, the latter had certainly bested the Austrians. It seemed to the Germans, therefore, that any future Austrian offensive would need their help if it was to be successful.

The German failure to break through at Ypres on the Western Front in November 1914 caused a change of strategy. Erich von Falkenhayn, the German chief-of-staff, decided to go on the defensive in the West and attack in the East. A number of German divisions were transferred from France and Flanders to the Eastern Front. A joint Austro-German offensive was planned for early 1915. This would aim to clear the Russians from East Prussia and, in the south, drive them away from the Carpathians and lift the siege of the fortress of Przemysl.

The Carpathian offensive opened in mid-January, but made little progress in the deep snow and was stopped after less than two weeks. Besieged Przemysl eventually surrendered in March.

The offensive in East Prussia went better, with some 90,000 men of the Russian Tenth Army being taken prisoner. But the Russians displayed remarkable resilience, summoning up another army that counter-attacked, bringing the offensive to a halt.

Between the trenches are any amount of dead and decomposing bodies of our own men and Turks lying on the heather. The smell is awful.

CAPTAIN GUY NIGHTINGALE

Von Hindenburg wanted to strike once more from East Prussia, but the Austrian chief-of-staff, Conrad von Hoetzendorf, argued that it was on the southern flank of the Polish salient that the potential for decisive action remained. Von Falkenhayn was the arbiter and came down in favour of the Austrian proposal.

Two other theatres of war had opened. After much German persuasion, Turkey entered the war on the side of the Central Powers. This provoked war with Russia, and the Turks decided to thrust into the Caucasus and foment a rising in Georgia. The Russians brought in reinforcements and counter-attacked, driving the Turks back with the loss of 75 per cent of their troops.

The Caucasus situation triggered another campaign when the Grand Duke Nicholas asked the Western Allies to do something to remove the Turkish threat to this region. The result was the Anglo-French expedition to the Dardanelles. Initially, during February and March 1915, only warships were used to force a way through the narrows and into the Black Sea, but they were eventually foiled by mines. On 25 April landings were carried out by British, Australian and French troops. Losses were high, but they managed to secure a number of toeholds. Thereafter, the campaign degenerated into another bitter and bloody stalemate. Eventually, the Allies withdrew in early January 1916.

May 1915 saw the Austrians committed to a new campaign, when Italy – under pressure from the British and French, and bent on annexing the southern Tirol – declared war on her northern neighbour. For the next two and a half years, neither side was able to make any significant progress, although not for want of trying. For the Germans this meant that they would have to send further troops to bolster their ally.

That same month of May 1915 also witnessed the opening of the Austro-German spring offensive against the Russians. Fourteen divisions attacked south of the River Vistula, between Gorlice and Tarnow, and immediately sent the Russians reeling back across the River San. Przemysl was regained and Lemberg fell. It looked as though the Russians might finally crack, especially when in July von Hindenburg joined in from East Prussia, entering

Warsaw the following month. Yet in spite of overwhelming losses, Russian resilience held up. The Tsar took personal command and by October the Russian armies had taken up a new and shorter defence line stretching from Riga on the Baltic to Czsernowitz on the Romanian border. This prevented any further Austro-German penetration.

After the disastrous Austrian invasion of Serbia in 1914, the Balkans remained quiet for most of 1915, but in October Bulgaria joined the Central Powers and, in conjunction with

Austrian and German forces, struck at Serbia. The Serbs were forced into a retreat. The British and French hastily rushed troops to Salonika in an effort to bolster the Serbs, but it was too late. The Austrians then turned on Montenegro and Albania, over-running both early in 1916.

So the beginning of 1916 found the Central Powers very much in the ascendant in the east. To restore Allied fortunes in 1916 attacks were called for on all fronts. The Germans decided to concentrate their attention on the West.

The main Russian contribution to the 1916 Allied strategy of attacks on all fronts was placed in the hands of General Alexei Brusilov. He recognised that the Central Powers' comprehensive rail network enabled them to deploy reserves quickly to any threatened point. Brusilov therefore decided to attack on a wide front in order to keep these reserves tied down. He chose, too, to strike at the Austrians rather than the Germans.

Brusilov opened his attack on 4 June, quickly tearing a great hole in the Austrian defences and advancing steadily towards the Carpathians in the south and the River Bug in the north. The Austrians appeared to be on the point of breaking and the Germans, who were now heavily committed at both Verdun and on the Somme on the Western Front, had to scrabble desperately to gather reserves to stop the rot.

(ABOVE) Russian troops advance during their successful invasion of Turkish Armenia in January 1916. The fighting on this front between the Russian and Ottoman Empires is little remembered. In the winter of 1914 the Russians successfully repulsed a Turkish assault and just over a year later launched their own offensive.

Encouraged by Brusilov's success, Romania declared war on the Central Powers at the end of August, which was to be a fatal decision. For by this time the Russian offensive had slowed through lack of reserves and supplies. The Germans struck the northern flank of the Russian salient and, although they were held, Brusilov decided that his position was now too vulnerable and withdrew to his original line. German, Austro-Hungarian and Bulgarian forces now turned on isolated Romania, and by the end of the year she was left with just the northern province of Moldavia.

By the end of 1916 the strain of war on the Russian state was becoming unbearable. The economy had collapsed, with all industry – apart from that directly supporting the war effort – at a standstill. Agriculture was suffering from loss of both manpower and draught animals to the war effort. Famine threatened.

The Bolsheviks and other revolutionaries fanned the flames of this discontent. The Russian Navy provided especially fertile ground because many months of relative inactivity

in port had bred boredom and discontent. In autumn 1916 there were mutinies in both the Baltic and Black Sea Fleets.

The indecisive, weak-willed Tsar and his entourage became increasingly isolated and reacted to the threat of revolution with greater repression. The situation was worsened by the baleful influence Grigori Rasputin had over the Tsarina. In desperation, some of his closest followers even began secretly negotiating with the Germans, in the belief that only ending the war would remove the growing threat to the throne. Others had Rasputin murdered on the night of 30 December 1916 in Petrograd, as St Petersburg had been called since 1914.

The Tsar continued to ignore all calls for reform and for a new government more sympathetic to the people's plight. There was a rapid rise in the numbers of striking workers and tension grew. In early March the Russian parliament, the Duma, met amid increasingly vociferous demonstrations. The Tsar, who had gone to his headquarters at the front, ordered the unrest to be quelled by force and for the Duma to be dissolved. Neither step was successful in restoring order and, significantly, members of the military garrison of Petrograd joined the demonstrators.

The Duma formed a Provisional Committee to try to restore order. At the same time a new body came into being, the Petrograd Soviet of Workers' and Soldiers' Deputies, dedicated to forming a parliament based on 'universal, equal, secret and direct suffrage'. The Tsar attempted to return to Petrograd by train, but was diverted by revolutionaries. Now totally isolated, he accepted that he had to abdicate. This he did on 15 March 1917, handing over the throne to his brother, the Grand Duke Michael, who declined to accept it. Five days later Nicholas and his family were arrested. The Russian monarchy was at an end.

A Provisional Government was now formed. This represented all shades of political opinion, but the Petrograd Soviet remained a separate body, and this would cause increasing difficulties.

At the same time, the Provisional Government assured the Western Allies that Russia would continue to play her part in the war. The Petrograd Soviet, on the other hand, called for all the warring nations to renounce their aggressive aims and make an early peace. These calls for an end to the fighting began to infiltrate the Russian Army by means of agitators within its ranks.

The Germans were well aware of the turmoil within Russia, and were keen to exploit the situation. The main Bolshevik leader, Vladimir Ilyich Ulyanov, better known as Lenin, had been in exile since the 1905 revolution, and was now domiciled in Switzerland. Lenin wanted Russia out of the war and so, in April 1917, the Germans arranged for Lenin to be taken secretly by train to Russia, travelling via Sweden and Finland, in order to bind the forces of revolution and make certain that this happened.

When I asked them what they wanted now they said they did not want to fight anymore and pleaded to be allowed to go home . . . and live in freedom.

GENERAL ALEXEI BRUSILOV:
RUSSIAN CHIEF-OF-STAFF

Thirty-six-year-old Alexander Kerensky now dominated the Russian Provisional Government as minister of war. He believed that a military victory was the best means of overcoming the unrest in the country. He brought in Brusilov, who had masterminded the summer 1916 offensive, as commander-in-chief. The two of them now planned another major offensive using the less disaffected formations.

The idea was to strike into Galicia once more, with attacks north and south of the River Dniester. But while more guns and shells were available for this than in any previous Russian offensive, other preparations were thin in the extreme, with no effort being made to prepare jump-off positions. The Austrians and Germans were well aware that the offensive was going to take place.

The offensive began on 1 July after a two-day bombardment, which was largely ineffective against well-prepared defences. In sectors held by the Germans, the first line was thinly held and so there was initial success, but when the Russians came up against the second line they suffered. South of the Dniester, the Austro-Hungarian defences were less robust and the Russians succeeded in driving a wedge between two armies. But the same difficulty that the Russians had experienced in 1916 now resurfaced. They lacked the necessary reserves to maintain the momentum of their attacks. In contrast, their enemies were able to deploy theirs quickly to threatened points.

By 16 July the Russians had been halted everywhere. Three days later they faced a counter-offensive. Russian troops fled in panic, many deserting. Only when they reached the old border with Austro-Hungary did they recover. Special 'death battalions' rounded up deserters and shot or hanged them. This and other draconian measures enabled the armies to prevent any further advance by the Central Powers.

Back in Petrograd, Lenin attempted a coup in July, but Kerensky was able to snuff it out with the help of some loyal troops hastily

(ABOVE) Russian wounded being brought back from the Front during the autumn of 1917. The collapse of morale and massive losses during the final Russian offensive and the German counterattacks meant that the army was no longer an effective fighting force.

brought back from the front. Lenin was now forced to go into hiding and slipped away to Finland, while Kerensky took over as head of the Provisional Government. In order to try to contain the growing anarchy that was engulfing the country, Kerensky turned to General Lavrenti Kornilov, whom he had appointed as commander-in-chief in place of Brusilov. But Kerensky was misinformed that Kornilov wanted the dissolution of the government and was demanding that all power should be placed in his hands. In September 1917 Kerensky had Kornilov arrested, thereby losing the general support of the officer corps. In the meantime, in what was to be their final attack, the Germans captured Riga, Russia's second largest Baltic port, using the stormtroop tactics that the Western Allies were to face in the spring of 1918. Many Russian soldiers refused to fight and merely withdrew.

Lenin and his Bolsheviks were waiting in the wings. Crucial to their success was winning over, or at least neutralising, the 350,000 men who made up the Petrograd Military District. This task was given to one Leon Trotsky, who discovered that the Provisional Government intended to send the majority of these troops to the front, although few were willing to go.

For all its failings and for all its problems, the Imperial Russian Army had to the end held down 160 German and Austrian divisions. These were now free to be released and the effect of this on the Allied war effort was absolutely devastating.

CHRIS BELLAMY,
HISTORIAN:
INTERVIEWED FOR THE PROGRAMME

The task was thus relatively simple, with only two regiments refusing to be suborned.

On 30 October Lenin returned clandestinely from Finland. A Revolutionary Military Committee was set up and sent commissars to each regiment and ship. Not until the very eve of the revolution did the Provisional Government wake up to what was happening. In the early hours of 6 November the Petrograd Military District began to order loyal units, including a women's battalion and officer cadet units, to Petrograd. The cruiser *Aurora*, moored on the River Neva, which runs through Petrograd, was ordered back to her base at Kronstadt to prevent her guns being used by the revolutionaries.

Early on 7 November Kerensky began frantic telephoning to get more troops into the city from outlying garrisons, especially Cossacks, who were known to be anti-Bolshevik. Their morale was as low as most other units, however, and their response was slow. In the meantime, the revolutionaries seized key points in the city. By mid-morning Kerensky was desperate, and decided to go by car to the headquarters of the northern armies to obtain loyal troops. He left, leaving the Provisional Government in session in the Winter Palace, and never returned.

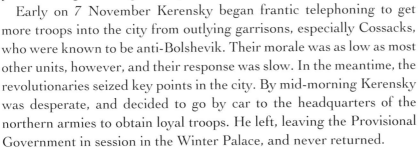

It was the Winter Palace which now became the centre of attention. The Government resisted surrender demands. That evening the cruiser *Aurora*, which had not sailed, began to bombard the palace. By 11 p.m. the revolutionaries broke down the gates and charged into the palace. Searching room by room, they eventually came across the ministers of the Provisional Government and arrested them. The revolution had been victorious.

A few days later Moscow also succumbed, but in most other places the revolutionaries failed. It was therefore going to take much fighting to bring Russia under their control.

Meanwhile, the country was still at war with the Central Powers. Overtures were made to Germany and an armistice came into force on the Eastern Front in mid-December. This enabled the Germans to begin transferring troops over to the Western Front in order to launch an offensive against the Western Allies before the American presence in France became too strong.

Indeed, one of Russia's allies was already feeling the effects of the release of men from the Eastern Front. On 24 October 1917 Austrian and German divisions successfully attacked the Italian armies in northeast Italy. After a few days Italian withdrawal had become a retreat and then almost a rout. Not until they reached the River Piave, a bare 15 miles from Venice, were the Italians able to stabilise the situation. In response to their frantic pleas, Britain and France were forced to send 11 divisions from France in order to bolster their defences.

As for a peace treaty between Russia and the Central Powers, the Bolsheviks wanted it to be based on the principle of no territorial annexation, but the Germans and Austrians insisted that this must not apply to Poland or the Baltic states and Finland. Furthermore, a Ukrainian delegation entered the stage, determined to gain independence. The Central Powers signed a separate treaty with Ukraine in early February 1918, which gave them access to Ukrainian grain. The Bolsheviks did not like this, or the prospect of the loss of Finland and the Baltic states, and tried to play for time. The Central Powers' patience soon ran out. They denounced the armistice and began to advance into the Ukraine. The Bolsheviks, desperate to re-employ the troops in securing the revolution, were forced to cave in and signed the Treaty of Brest-Litovsk on 3 March. Its terms were worse than originally envisaged in that Russia also had to cede the southern Caucasus to Turkey. Furthermore, the Germans and Austrians continued their advance and occupied the entire Ukraine. Romania, Russia's one eastern ally, was now totally isolated and also forced to surrender. The peace that the Bolsheviks signed was therefore humiliating, but bringing the rest of Russia under their sway was uppermost in their minds, especially since they only effectively controlled a narrow corridor between Petrograd and Moscow. Indeed, what was to be a long and bloody civil war had already begun.

WAR ON THE EASTERN FRONT

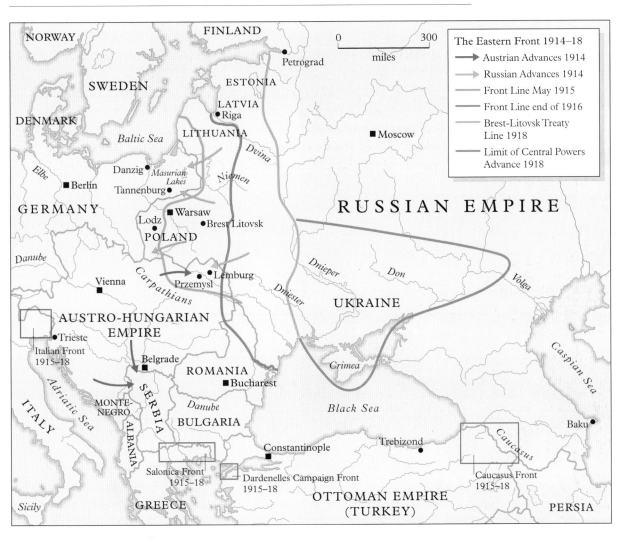

The Eastern Front 1914–18
- Austrian Advances 1914
- Russian Advances 1914
- Front Line May 1915
- Front Line end of 1916
- Brest-Litovsk Treaty Line 1918
- Limit of Central Powers Advance 1918

After the October Revolution and the armistice the Allies decided to give support to the anti-Bolshevik forces in the hope of bringing Russia back into the war. Consequently, early in 1918, the British and French naval presence in the Russian Arctic ports was increased and Japanese, American and British warships were also sent to the Far Eastern port of Vladivostok. This was the beginning of the Allied intervention that would add another dimension to the agonies of the Russian Civil War.

(TOP) After their victory at Tannenberg in August 1914, the Germans were quick to take the offensive, thrusting into Russian-controlled Poland towards Warsaw. The fighting swept back and forth until the city was finally seized in August 1915.

(MIDDLE) Hardy and stoical Russian infantry during the winter of 1914–15. When the war began the Tsar's forces were described as 'unfit for modern war', but the fighting quality of the badly led and inadequately equipped 'Russian steamroller' surprised the Germans.

(BOTTOM) The quality of the equipment of the Russian forces improved steadily during the first 18 months of the war. A gigantic industrial effort had begun which, by 1916, ensured that almost every Russian soldier had a rifle and that there were adequate shells and artillery.

ON THE PLAINS AND IN THE FORESTS OF EASTERN EUROPE THREE GREAT
EMPIRES GRAPPLED IN A SERIES OF TITANIC BUT LITTLE KNOWN BATTLES.

*There was no doubt that, despite their terrific
losses, the Russians would soon resume their
offensive . . . . They had plenty of men, but
used them recklessly.*

GENERAL ERICH LUDENDORFF,
MEMOIR

(ABOVE) A priest blesses
troops during the winter
fighting in early 1915. At this
stage the men died willingly for
their 'Little Father' the Tsar. It
was the incompetence of much
of the officer corps and the
corruption of the military
bureaucracy which were the
main drawbacks.

THE ENTRY OF TURKEY INTO THE WAR
SEEMED TO OFFER AN OPPORTUNITY TO
BREAK THE STALEMATE ON THE
WESTERN FRONT.

(LEFT) Winston Churchill, First Lord of the Admiralty, was a leading enthusiast for the idea of helping Russia by knocking out Turkey with an assault in the Dardanelles to seize Constantinople.

(BOTTOM LEFT) Turkish crowds seem surprised that their country is at war. There was little obvious benefit for them, whereas the Turkish empire in the Eastern Mediterranean and Middle East offered all sorts of possibilities for Allied action.

(RIGHT) French battleships in action in the Dardanelles. The attempt by an Allied fleet of 14 British capital ships and four French to force this narrow strait and reach Constantinople was thwarted by minefields and Turkish artillery. Three ships were sunk and three put out of action before it was decided that troops would have to capture the Gallipoli peninsula.

THE TURKS SOON FOUND THEMSELVES HARD-PRESSED ON EVERY FRONT,
FROM HIGH SNOWCAPPED MOUNTAINS TO DESERTS. THEY WON ONLY ONE
CLEAR VICTORY.

(TOP LEFT) British troops
landing at Gallipoli. The
campaign proved a disaster and
they were pulled out nine
months later, having suffered
213,900 casualties – 145,000 to
sickness and 15,000 to
frostbite. The reality was that
never enough men or
equipment were available to
pull off such a complex
operation against a determined
enemy who held high ground.

(BOTTOM LEFT) Turkish
artillery in action in Palestine.
Wherever they fought the
Turkish troops earned the
respect of their enemies for
courage and determination. But
attempts to threaten the Suez
Canal were easily thwarted by
British troops, while the Arabs
were inspired to revolt by
Lawrence of Arabia.

(ABOVE) Russian troops on
Bactrian camels during their
campaign against a Turkish
attempt to invade the Caucasus
in winter 1914. In this little-
known campaign the Russians
were triumphantly successful,
destroying three-quarters of
the Turkish army. In January
1916, in the same region, the
Russians were equally
successful when they invaded
Turkish Armenia.

IN 1916 UNDER A COMPETENT COMMANDER THE RUSSIAN FORCES LAUNCHED AN OFFENSIVE WHICH HURLED THE ENEMY BACK IN DISARRAY.

(ABOVE) General Alexei Brusilov inspects the enemy front. One of the war's most underrated commanders he launched a highly successful offensive against the Austrians in Galicia in June 1916. This used many startling new methods – among them a short, highly accurate preliminary bombardment.

(TOP LEFT) Austrian prisoners being brought in under guard. Well led and properly equipped for once, the Russian army performed excellently. Emerging from carefully concealed positions and tunnels dug under their own wire they swiftly overran the Austrian defences and swept forward up to 50 miles on a 200-mile front.

(BOTTOM LEFT) Well-deserved medals being awarded during Brusilov's offensive. In nine days his men had killed over 60,000 of the enemy and captured more than 190,000. Over the next two months of fighting the Austrians and Germans suffered more than 750,000 casualties, and the Habsburg Empire was close to collapse.

IN MAY 1915 ITALY JOINED THE WAR, HOPING TO REGAIN THE PROVINCES WHICH HAD BEEN OCCUPIED BY THE HABSBURGS. BUT THE CAMPAIGN WAS NOT AS EASY AS HAD BEEN HOPED.

(ABOVE) Austrian officers inspect the Alpine terrain in which the war was fought. Although outnumbered about eight to one by the Italian army, they had the inestimable advantage of holding the heights and no urgent reason to take the offensive.

Everything froze hard during the night . . . and the lather froze on one's face before one had time to shave

LIEUTENANT HUGH DALTON,
MEMOIR

(TOP) The fighting in the Italian campaign took place in some of the most hostile and difficult conditions in the world. Even in summer some of the action took place close to the snow line, and in winter the Italians were faced almost everywhere by precipitate slopes covered in snow and sheet ice.

(MIDDLE) Italian troops carrying dismantled artillery up a mountain path. Every piece of equipment had to be manhandled up the mountainside, making preparations for an offensive extremely difficult. The Isonzo area in which much of the fighting took place was described as a 'howling wilderness with stones as sharp as knives'.

(BOTTOM) Kaiser Wilhelm II, dressed in an Austrian field marshal's uniform greets the Austrian chief-of-staff Conrad von Hoetzendorf. For the first two and a half years the Germans were content to let the Italian Front take care of itself. They knew that fighting the Italians was one of the few things that united all races in the Habsburg Empire.

THE CONSTANT DEMANDS FOR OFFENSIVE ACTION TOOK A DREADFUL TOLL ON THE ITALIAN TROOPS. WHEN THE ENEMY FINALLY TURNED, THEY WERE UNABLE TO MEET THE CHALLENGE.

(TOP LEFT) The Italian commander, Count Luigi Cadorna. Described as 'the arch-attritionist' he launched 11 offensives in the Isonzo area, causing far more casualties to his men than to the enemy. In the 11th battle more than 166,000 died in 11 days.

(BOTTOM LEFT) Austrian troops manhandling a heavy machine-gun. The collapse of Russia in autumn 1917 allowed the Austrians to reinforce the Italian front along with seven German divisions. At the Battle of Caporetto on 25 October the Italians forces collapsed.

(ABOVE) British troops crossing a pontoon bridge. Five British and six French divisions had to be sent from the Western Front to steady the Italian line. By the time they got there, the exhausted Austrians and Germans had ground to a halt at the River Piave.

WITHIN SIX MONTHS OF BRUSILOV'S WONDERFUL VICTORY, A DISHEARTENED AND EMBITTERED RUSSIA COLLAPSED INTO REVOLUTION.

(ABOVE) An agitator distributes leaflets to soldiers and civilians during the autumn of 1916. Brusilov's offensive turned out to be the Tsarist regime's last throw. By 1917 Russia had suffered more than five million casualties and confidence in the government had begun to ebb away.

(TOP RIGHT) Conscripts being called up in early 1916. Many were taken from the new industries that had grown up during the war in which criticism of the regime was rampant. (BOTTOM RIGHT) A bread queue in St Petersburg during the winter of 1916–17.

(TOP LEFT) The Tsar and Tsarevich inspect Cossack officers during the winter of 1916–17. He had taken direct command of the army in September 1915 and was now being personally blamed for all Russia's problems. When food riots began in St Petersburg on the 11 March he immediately gave into demands for a new provisional government, and then abdicated on the 15th.

(BOTTOM LEFT) Crowds at a demonstration in St Petersburg. Chaos and violence reigned as the abdication of the Tsar unleashed enormous and conflicting demands for reform and effectively ended what little popular support there was for continuing the war.

WHEN THE COLLAPSE OF THE TSAR'S REGIME CAME, IT WAS AMAZINGLY SWIFT AND TOTAL.

(TOP) Alexander Kerensky, who was appointed Minister for War in May 1917. He joined with General Brusilov in attempting to launch another offensive against the Germans and Austrians in July, but the troops refused to fight.

(BOTTOM) Bodies of the fallen are paraded through the streets of Moscow in the autumn of 1917. Following up the effective collapse of the Russian army, the Germans had occupied all of Poland and advanced deep into the Ukraine and the Baltic states.

A NEW FACE APPEARS IN ST PETERSBURG, AND
THE HISTORY OF RUSSIA IS CHANGED FOREVER.

(ABOVE) Disaffected officers addressing a crowd in St Petersburg. In August Kerensky appointed himself Prime Minister of the Provisional Government. He was still determined to keep Russia in the war and put down the chaos at home. But a new and determined focus had now appeared for the anti-war movement.

(RIGHT) Vladimir Ulyanov, leader of the minority Bolshevik faction of the Russian Communist Party and better known as Lenin. He had spent more than 16 years in exile and returned to Russia in April 1917. He was implacably opposed to the Provisional Government, rejected any form of 'bourgeois democracy', and was determined that Russia must leave the war.

ONCE THE BOLSHEVIKS HAD SEIZED POWER, RUSSIA SWIFTLY COLLAPSED
INTO CIVIL WAR AND THE TSAR WAS DOOMED.

(TOP LEFT) Lenin meets the people. He misjudged the support for his anti-war message and fled abroad again after an abortive coup in July. But by September his Bolsheviks had achieved majorities on the ruling councils of St Petersburg and Moscow, and in October he launched a successful coup.

(BOTTOM LEFT) While Russia collapsed, the Germans kept up the pressure. By the end of the year they had received their reward. The new Bolshevik government hurried to make peace in December 1917 at Brest-Litovsk, and the Germans were free at last from the fear of war on two fronts.

(ABOVE) The Tsar with his wife, son and two of his four daughters, posing with Cossack officers during the winter of 1916. Within a few weeks the Tsar would have abdicated. Imprisoned by the Provisional Government and then by the Bolsheviks, the Imperial family's existence was seen as a threat to the revolution.

THIS IS THE STORY OF 1918

—

THE YEAR THAT CHANGED EVERYTHING

6 WAR TO END ALL WAR?

1918 and the Aftermath

Whatever happens, we must obtain peace before the enemy breaks through into Germany: if he does, woe on us.

CROWN PRINCE RUPRECHT OF BAVARIA,
ARMY GROUP COMMANDER, 18 OCTOBER

The first half of 1918 had not generally gone well for the Western Allies. The worst event had been the formal exit of Russia from the war in March 1918, which enabled the Germans to concentrate the bulk of their forces in the West and then deal the Allies a series of near-devastating blows. Yet, by the middle of July, the Allies had managed to exhaust Germany's offensive capability. Crucially, there were now 300,000 American troops in France and more were arriving at a rate of well over 250,000 per month. The French Marshal Ferdinand Foch, the Allied Generalissimo, was thus determined to attack before the Germans could recover from their exertions of the past four months.

The arrival of the Americans had given the tired British and French a much-needed shot in the arm. The Allies desperately needed help to relieve them of some of the exhausting burden of the Western Front. In April 1917, however, the American Regular Army had only some 110,000 men under arms, augmented by 150,000 National Guardsmen. Furthermore, these troops were hardly trained for the type of war being fought in Europe. As far as tanks and artillery, machine-guns and mortars, and combat aircraft were concerned, the American troops would have to be largely equipped by the British and French.

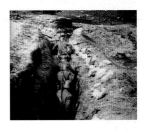

Also, only once they arrived in France could they be properly trained in modern warfare. Finally, the 1916 mobilisation of the National Guard had revealed a serious shortfall in the number of men reporting for duty. As a result limited conscription had to be imposed. It would be some time before the American presence could make itself felt on the Western Front.

General John Pershing, popularly known as 'Black Jack', commanded the American Expeditionary Force. He was determined to maintain the entity of the American forces in France, rather than allow them to fight piecemeal under French and British command, even during the dark days of spring 1918 when the Germans seemed to be driving all before them. Pershing declared the formation of the First United States Army of 14 divisions. It was now to play its part in the final Allied offensive.

The tide was turning on the other war fronts. Stiffened by French and British troops, the Italians recovered after the disaster of Caporetto in autumn 1917. In the latter half of October 1918, the Allies struck across the River Piave in such a devastating way as to split the Austrian armies, throw them back in confusion, and force them to ask for an armistice after just over two weeks' fighting. Likewise, the deadlock in Salonika between the Allied forces and the Bulgarians was finally broken, with another autumn offensive quickly forcing Bulgaria to throw in the towel.

The Middle East had seen two long campaigns between the British and Turks. In Mesopotamia, now Iraq, Indian troops had landed at Basra in November 1914 in order to secure the oilfields in the region. An advance up the River Tigris almost as far as Baghdad was then made, but logistical support had been lacking. The British force withdrew, but was then besieged and forced to surrender at Kut el Amara in April 1916. A fresh commander and wholesale reorganisation resulted in another advance, which reached Baghdad exactly a year later. The British forces continued to push further north and even reached Baku on the Caspian Sea.

In early 1915 the Turks had made an abortive attack across the Suez Canal into Egypt. There followed a virtual stalemate until the end of 1916, when the British crossed the Canal and began to advance into Sinai. In the autumn of 1917, the British managed to break through the Turkish defences and entered Jerusalem. Demands for reinforcements to help hold back the German drives on the Western Front forced an interruption, and it was not until autumn 1918 that the offensive was renewed. By this time, the Turks were also facing an Arab revolt in their rear, which had been largely fomented by a British officer, T. E. Lawrence. The Turks sued for peace at the end of October.

The South Africans had had little difficulty in seizing German south-west Africa early in the war. The German colonies in West Africa were also overrun relatively quickly, but

The discipline of the German Army is quickly going, and the German Officer is no longer what he was. It seems to me to be the beginning of the end.

FIELD MARSHAL SIR DOUGLAS HAIG,
10 SEPTEMBER 1918

not so in German east Africa. The German commander, Paul von Lettow-Vorbeck, proved to be a highly skilled commander. With a force of never more than 20,000 men, most of them locally raised Askaris, he kept six times as many British, Indian and African troops at bay for four years.

The centre of the war was still the Western Front. Foch's plan was for the Allies to keep striking in turn in order to allow the Germans no respite. First came the counter-offensive into flanks of the German salients in Champagne. Then, on 8 August, the British struck at Amiens. Spearheaded by tanks and armoured cars, Australian and Canadian troops broke through the German defences in one day. Ludendorff, the German chief-of-staff, later described this as 'the Black Day for the German Army'. Subsequently, however, not enough tanks were available to maintain the momentum of the attack. In mid-September it was the turn of the Americans. They successfully eradicated the St Mihiel salient east of Verdun. Then the Belgians and British attacked out of the Ypres salient. Now the French and Americans struck in the broken and hilly country of Argonne.

At the beginning of October the British broke through the Hindenburg Line and were now fighting in open country. It took time to adjust to this more fluid form of warfare after years spent in the trenches, and the German rearguards fought fiercely.

The German ability to fight was seemingly unimpaired, but behind the front there were growing doubts as to Germany's ability to continue the war. The Allied blockade had been very tight for a long time and food was becoming desperately short. Front-line troops were now subsisting on black bread, coffee made of acorns, bad potatoes and horsemeat, but for the civilians at home it was much worse. Germany was also beginning to run out of manpower, with 17- and even 16-year-olds being conscripted. It was not only the Germans at home who were beginning to realise that defeat was staring them in the face; even Ludendorff had, by the beginning of October, accepted that the war was lost. He

WAR TO END ALL WAR? **189**

recommended an immediate withdrawal to Germany's 1914 western borders and that overtures should be made to the Allies for an armistice.

This approach was to be initiated on the basis of a declaration made by President Woodrow Wilson in January 1918, and agreed by his allies, on conditions for peace. The so-called Fourteen Points not only demanded the surrender of all territory seized by the Central Powers during the war, but also the return of Alsace-Lorraine, which Prussia had taken from France in 1870, and the break-up of the Austro-Hungarian and Ottoman empires, with their varied ethnic groupings being granted the right to self-determination. Poland, too, was to gain her independence.

In order to make Wilson more sympathetic, a new, more liberal German chancellor, Prince Max of Baden, was appointed, and a true parliamentary system of government instituted. Prince Max and the Austrians sent notes to Wilson on 4 October. Wilson reiterated the Fourteen Points, and Berlin accepted them on 12 October. Four days later, however, Wilson suddenly backtracked. His allies insisted that it was up to the military commanders to lay down the armistice terms. This they did, insisting that they must be such as to make it impossible for Germany to renew hostilities. This implied surrender and threw Berlin, which had been hoping for peace with honour, into confusion.

Germany's allies now began to desert her. Bulgaria had already signed an armistice at the end of September, Turkey did so on 30 October, and then Austro-Hungary on 4 November.

The German Government, isolated and under intense pressure from below – pressure that seemed to have all the hallmarks of an incipient revolution – finally accepted that the armistice had to be on Allied terms. Ludendorff, who suddenly began to view the military situation in a more favourable light and called for a renewed effort to avoid a dishonourable peace, was sacked. This did not appease left-wing elements. They demanded an immediate end to hostilities and called a general strike in Berlin.

On 7 November the Germans informed Marshal Foch of the names of those constituting their armistice delegation, who were all civilians, a fact that was later to be of much significance. Foch made it clear that the terms for the armistice, which included immediate withdrawal from conquered territory, Allied occupation of the west bank of the Rhine and bridgeheads beyond it, and the immediate surrender of vast amounts of war *matériel*, were non-negotiable. Conscious of the rising domestic pressures, the German delegates had no option but to accept them.

. . . the tremendous joy and relief that the war finally had come to an end dominated our emotions completely. Whatever awaited us from now on in civilian life would be easy by comparison. I was not at all afraid of the future.

LIEUTENANT FRITZ NAGEL,
Memoir

At 5 a.m. on 11 November 1918, as the guns continued to thunder on the Western Front, the German delegation signed the armistice document in a railway carriage in the Forest of Compiegne. Six hours later the guns ceased their angry rumbling. In all, ten million men lost their lives as a direct result of the war.

Germany, meanwhile, was in turmoil. Its new democratic government was quickly under threat from the hard left, in the shape of the Soldiers' and Workers' Councils and the even more extreme Spartacists, followers of Lenin bent on installing a communist regime. There were also the sailors who had mutinied at the end of October, who now formed the People's Naval Division, which deployed to Berlin. The government itself tried to steer a middle course, forming its own military units for its protection rather than be seen to be supported by the army of the old order. It also promised new elections.

Matters came to a head at the beginning of January 1919, after there had been clashes with government troops just before Christmas. The Spartacists declared the government to be at an end and called a general strike. By this stage, though, a number of German army officers returning from the front with their troops had become so concerned by the growing anarchy that they formed volunteer units known as Freikorps. It was to these that the government was forced to turn, and they quickly moved in and crushed the Spartacists, killing their two leaders, Rosa Luxembourg and Karl Liebknecht. Even so, similar turmoil erupted elsewhere in Germany.

The government kept its promise to hold elections and won them. It then moved out of Berlin, to the little town of Weimar, 150 miles to the south-west, where security would be easier to maintain. This, however, did not halt the unrest, which culminated in a general strike being declared throughout the country at the beginning of March. Once again the Freikorps moved into Berlin. In the space of ten days they crushed the revolution, forcing the German communists to go underground.

Germany, however, was by no means the only country that experienced political unrest during the immediate postwar period. The Austro-Hungarian Emperor, Karl, who had

succeeded to the throne after the death of Franz Joseph in 1916, abdicated, like the Kaiser, at the end of the war. Hungary immediately broke away and in February 1919 the recently installed democratic government was overthrown by Bela Kun, who had been indoctrinated into communism while a prisoner-of-war of the Russians. In turn, there was a successful right-wing counter-coup led by Admiral Miklos Horthy, who was to rule the country for almost 25 years.

In Russia the civil war had grown ever more widespread until it engulfed the country. At base it was the determination of the White or anti-Bolshevik forces to overthrow the revolution and that of its defenders, the Reds, to secure it.

In the spring of 1919 three White armies began to converge on the Red heartland based in Petrograd and Moscow in western Russia. From Siberia, where he had set up a White government, came Admiral Kolchak. Advancing north from the Ukraine was General Denikin, and from Estonia came General Yudenich. But other elements were also involved. Controlling the Trans-Siberian railway with their armoured trains were 40,000 Czechs, former subjects of Vienna and prisoners of war, whose prime concern was to get home. They were therefore prepared to help Kolchak only so long as it was in their interest to do so. Likewise, the Cossacks, who wanted to set up an independent state, were prepared to help Denikin in the Ukraine as long as he was being successful. Baltic Germans also supported Yudenich, and German troops enabled the Finns to mount a counter-revolution and gain independence from Russia.

Yet another aspect of the war was the part played by the wartime Allies. Initially they had sent small contingents to Russia in the vain hope that she might continue to fight on against the Germans. Once Lenin had pulled Russia out of the war in March 1918, and the civil war intensified, their role changed to one of giving active support to the Whites because of fears that Bolshevism would destabilise western Europe. This was especially so after March 1919, with the general tide of unrest that swept much of the world and the founding of the Comintern in Moscow, an organisation dedicated to engineering the spread of communism. Thus, Japanese, American and British ground and naval forces were deployed to Vladivostok, British and French elements were present in the Ukraine and Caucasus, and British, French, Canadian, American, Italian and even Serbian forces were stationed in the extreme north, around the ports of Murmansk and Archangel.

With all this support the Whites should have overcome Bolshevism with comparative ease, but this was not to be the case. The White commanders were generally inept and there was little cooperation among them. Many of the soldiers they commanded proved to be ill-disciplined and unreliable. The Reds, on the other hand,

(ABOVE) British troops bringing in prisoners during the great Allied offensives that finally broke the German Army. By the autumn of 1918 the Germans had effectively run out of manpower with which to replace the 1–2 million casualties that they had suffered since Ludendorff began his attack in March.

had as their military leader Leon Trotsky, who proved himself to be a natural organiser and inspirational leader. Through his numerous visits to the various fronts, he was able to inspire his soldiers. His intricate web of political commissars also ensured that they were instilled with the necessary discipline. Communications, too, were very much better in western Russia than elsewhere. Consequently, he was able to defeat each of the White armies in turn and by early 1920 the Reds were victorious everywhere. The Allies had seen the writing on the wall well before then, and had faced increasing domestic questioning over their role in Russia. They, therefore, withdrew their support for the Whites.

The main victims of the Russian Civil War were the ordinary people. Not only were they subjected to barbarities of every sort by both Reds and Whites, but the war totally disrupted industry, communications and agriculture. This resulted in widespread famine and disease. No one knows how many perished, but the total certainly ran into several millions.

If I were the Germans I shouldn't sign for a moment. You see it gives them no hope whatsoever, either now or in the future.

HAROLD NICOLSON:
BRITISH DIPLOMAT, 1919

In January 1919 representatives of the Allied nations met in Paris and began to decide on the peace terms. While all agreed with President Wilson's January 1918 Fourteen Points as principles for avoiding future wars, there was initially much divergence in views as to the degree to which the defeated nations, who were seen as the original aggressors, should be punished. France could not forget the one and a half million dead she had suffered and the devastation in the northern part of her land. Consequently, her prime minister, Georges Clemenceau, was especially keen to make Germany pay for the damage she had caused. British Prime Minister David Lloyd George had had to face an election in December 1918 and was returned to office on the slogan 'make Germany pay', his electorate conscious of their 760,000 dead and a massive financial debt to America. Wilson himself, whose Fourteen Points were far-sighted, was undermined by the fact that elections to both the Senate and the House of Representatives in November 1918 had returned majorities for the opposition Republicans, whose policy was to disengage from Europe as soon as possible. He was therefore in a weak position.

Of the 24 lesser powers who sent representatives to the peace conference, Italy and Japan were the most vociferous, but neither got all they wanted in terms of territorial rewards. Italy gained South Tirol, but not the east coast of the Adriatic. Japan was awarded former German islands in the Pacific, but no territory in mainland China.

Germany lost all her overseas possessions, which were given to Britain, France and Japan. The Ottoman Empire was broken up, with France being awarded the mandates of Syria and Lebanon, and Britain those of Palestine, Transjordan and Iraq. Within Europe itself, Wilson's principle of self-determination, one of the Fourteen Points, exerted a large influence. Three independent Baltic states, Latvia, Estonia and Lithuania, were created, and Poland gained her independence. She was awarded the whole of Galicia and, more significant for the future, a corridor to the Baltic in the Danzig (now Gdansk) area, thus isolating the German territory of East Prussia.

The remainder of the old Austro-Hungarian empire was entirely broken up, with Hungarian independence being recognised. A new state was created in the Balkans – Yugoslavia. This took in Serbia and Montenegro, and Austria's former Balkan provinces, including Croatia and Bosnia-Hercegovina. This suited the Serbs, since it gave them domination, but was also favourable to the other ethnic groupings since it transferred them from the losing to the winning side. The creation of this artificial state would, however, create problems with which the world is still wrestling to this day.

In order to prevent the conquered nations from waging aggressive war in the future, their armed forces and armaments were severely restricted. Germany was allowed only a standing all-volunteer army of 100,000 men, no large modern warships, no air force, no tanks and was restricted in the size of artillery guns. Furthermore, her armaments industry was to be largely dismantled and the Rhineland demilitarised. Even more crippling was that Germany had to pay huge financial reparations for the physical damage she had caused.

A strong body of opinion in Germany was in favour of rejecting the peace terms as being unbelievably harsh, arguing that her armies had not been defeated in the field. In truth, though, there was no option, and on 28 June 1919 the peace was signed in the Hall of Mirrors at Versailles, the very room in which Kaiser Wilhelm I had been proclaimed Emperor of all Germany in 1871. Peace treaties were subsequently signed with the other defeated states.

The Allies celebrated the Treaty of Versailles with victory parades in New York, Paris, London and elsewhere. Now they could turn to the business of dismantling their war machines and winning the peace, confident that they had taken the necessary steps to ensure that there would be no more major conflicts in Europe. The numerous war cemeteries and memorials that sprung up, together with the hundreds and thousands of people who had been physically and mentally mutilated as a result of 1914–18, also acted as a stark reminder of the horrors of war.

The Paris Peace Conference had, however, drawn up another way of ensuring that major conflict did not break out in the future. Again, the League of Nations was the brainchild of Woodrow Wilson. All victorious nations and neutral states were invited to join and 42 did so. It aimed to prevent potential conflict by arbitration. If this failed and one member did attack another, the League could impose sanctions and, as a last resort, force.

Yet, even as the League convened for the first time at its headquarters in Geneva, Switzerland, in November 1920, it was faced with problems. For a start, the US Senate had refused to ratify it. Worse, Wilson lost the presidential election in that same month, November, campaigning on a League platform. The American people had shown that once more they wanted to turn their backs on Europe. What this meant for the League was that it lost a major force and would be severely weakened.

The League, too, was born amid conflict. Initially this came from newly independent Poland, which was not wholly satisfied with the territorial awards made to it under the Versailles Treaty. In April 1920 Polish President Pilsudski declared a federation of Poland, Lithuania and the Ukraine, both of which had Polish minorities. Taking advantage of Russian weakness caused by the civil war, his troops invaded Ukraine in May and initially drove all before them, occupying Kiev. The Russians then struck back and, in turn, pushed the Poles back to the gates of Warsaw. Just when a Bolshevik tide seemed about to sweep westward, the Poles managed to snatch a devastating victory out of the jaws of defeat and in turn advanced once more into the Ukraine. A peace was eventually brokered in March 1921, with the Poles being allowed to keep most of their gains, territory that the Russians continued to regard as theirs.

There was trouble, too, with Turkey. The Allies had insisted that she surrender the extreme western part of Asia Minor, part of her mainland, so that her access from the Black Sea to the Mediterranean could be controlled. To this end Greek, Italian, and British troops were landed there. But while the Sultan of Turkey was prepared to accept this, some of his generals were not. One, Kemal Ataturk, raised an army and defeated and overthrew the Sultan in early 1921. The Italians now withdrew, and Kemal turned against the Greeks,

driving them back in disarray. The British at Chanak, at the eastern end of the Dardanelles Straits, remained in place without becoming embroiled before withdrawing in the autumn of 1922. The Allies then dropped their demands on the Turkish mainland and a revised peace treaty was signed.

The First World War was certainly tragic, but it wasn't futile. In the First World War the Allies achieved a great negative victory . . . They prevented the domination of Europe by militaristic Germany.

DR GARY SHEFFIELD,
KING'S COLLEGE LONDON

*I detached myself from the others and walked
slowly up Whitehall, with my heart sinking
in a sudden cold dismay. All those
with whom I had really been intimate were gone . . .
The War was over; a new age was beginning;
but the dead were dead and would never return.*

VERA BRITTAIN,
TESTAMENT OF YOUTH

The other means used to reduce the risk of war was disarmament.
Here the Americans were, in spite of their withdrawal from the League
of Nations, able to play a leading role. An early result was the Washington Naval Treaty of
1922. The major powers agreed to restrict not only the size of their navies in relation to each
other, but the size of their ships as well. An early and significant result of this was the
conversion of battleships then under construction to aircraft carriers.

Great efforts were made to ensure that the Great War would be the war to end all war.
But, as the immediate postwar decade moved on, resentment over the measures adopted to
achieve this would grow and new forces would emerge to threaten the world's peace.

As 1918 opened, the guns still thundered over the trenches. But both sides were convinced that the critical 'decisive blow' must be made.

(ABOVE) British gunners firing an 8-inch gun. By now the artillery was more than one-third of total British strength and its skills and experience had increased enormously. During the battles to come, its accuracy played a major part in stopping the German advance.

(RIGHT) French artillerymen loading a heavy howitzer. The French army always had far more artillery than the British – over 11,600 guns compared with 6,400. The batteries of the superb French 75-mm field gun required on average 280,000 shells a day.

Exactly as a pianist runs his hands across the keyboard from treble to bass, there rose in less than a minute the most tremendous cannonade I ever heard.

WINSTON CHURCHILL,
21 MARCH 1918

(TOP) German stormtroops preparing for an assault. These lightly armed and highly mobile units infiltrated the enemy lines behind a creeping barrage and aimed to penetrate deeply, leaving any strongpoints to be dealt with by follow-up infantry.

(MIDDLE) Exhausted German troops during Ludendorff's spring offensive. Their assault on 21 March 1918 caused the British more casualties on a single day than any other, except the first day of the Somme. In some places the Germans advanced more than ten miles, but Haig had planned his defence in depth.

(BOTTOM) British troops bringing in German prisoners during the follow-up attacks. Ludendorff launched four more attempts to break through the Allied line and, by June, his troops were within 50 miles of Paris. But by then the great bulge into the Allied line which had been created was very vulnerable to counter-attack.

THE GERMANS KNEW THEY HAD ONE LAST CHANCE TO DEFEAT THE ALLIES BEFORE AMERICA'S STRENGTH MADE THEM OVERWHELMING.

(ABOVE) German stormtroops using flamethrowers to overwhelm Allied front-line trenches. They made widespread use of this weapon – which had been first seen in 1915 – as well as grenades and the first machine pistols which had been developed for fighting in the close confines of trenches.

The turmoil of our feelings was called forth by rage, alcohol and thirst for blood as we stepped out, heavily yet irresistibly, for the enemy's lines . . .

LIEUTENANT ERNST JUNGER,
MEMOIR

FOR THE BRITISH FORCES IN PARTICULAR THE WESTERN FRONT WAS NOT THE ONLY KILLING GROUND.

(ABOVE) A British padre buries the dead during 1918. By the end of the war, the British Empire forces had suffered about a million dead. The great majority were on the Western Front, but troops were in action in many other places including the Middle and Far East and Africa.

(RIGHT) British troops marching through the Greek mountains near Salonika. One of the more pointless sideshows of the war was an Allied attempt to help Serbia in 1915. They failed and more than 50,000 men remained in what the Germans called 'the biggest internment camp of the war'.

We have seen real war in earnest now. It has been a terrible time but we remain unbeaten though exhausted, and the men are extraordinarily cheerful. It is heartbreaking to think of the fine fellows who have gone under.

LIEUTENANT COLONEL WALTER VIGNOBLES,
MEMOIR

By the autumn of 1918 the size of the US Army in France had swollen to 1.4 million troops, but preparing them for action had been slow.

(ABOVE) American troops practise firing a mortar while wearing gas masks. The majority of the troops who arrived in France had only been through basic training and needed a lot of extra work before they were ready for action. They also lacked any experienced field commanders at any level.

(TOP RIGHT) American troops training with French-built Renault tanks. The US army had also lacked any modern weaponry, and was to adopt its Allies' designs – everything from British helmets to French artillery and tanks.

(BOTTOM RIGHT) American troops moving up to the front. Their commander General Pershing's insistence that they must fight as a unified force delayed their entry into action.

BY MID-JULY 1918 THE GERMANS HAD REACHED THEIR LAST GASP. THEN
MARSHAL FERDINAND FOCH, THE ALLIED SUPREME COMMANDER LAUNCHED
HIS COUNTERSTROKE.

(ABOVE) Into the open at last. British troops advancing in July 1918. When the great Allied offensive began, three years of trench warfare meant that the British had little experience of mobile action. But they learnt fast.

(TOP RIGHT) A British Mark IV 'Male' tank with 6-pounder guns. One of the outstanding features of the Allied advance to victory was the increasingly close co-operation between all arms – artillery, tanks, infantry and aircraft.

(BOTTOM RIGHT) British troops freeing a bogged down motorbike and machine-gun sidecar. The limited technical resources of 1918 could not maintain the impetus of an advance across the wilderness of the earlier battlefields. Good progress was five miles a day.

AT LAST, IN SEPTEMBER 1918, THE US ARMY WAS READY TO TAKE THE FIELD IN ITS OWN BATTLE.

(TOP AND BOTTOM LEFT) US troops go over the top on 12 September 1918 to eliminate a German salient at St Mihiel. Their first battle of the war proved a swift success, but it was followed by a gruelling fight to clear the rugged, hilly and wooded Argonne Forest.

(ABOVE) US artillery firing in the open. The US forces suffered 117,000 casualties during the month of fighting in the Argonne, and were then kept out of the line until the final days of the war. By then the British 3rd and 4th Armies were on such a roll that Haig reported that their commanders had told him 'no further orders from me were necessary, and both would be able to carry on without difficulty!'

BY NOVEMBER 1918, THE 'MOTOR OF THE WAR', THE GERMAN ARMY HAD ALMOST TOTALLY RUN DOWN.

(TOP LEFT) German machine-gunners established themselves as the hard core of the defence. On 31 October 1918 Haig remarked: 'the enemy is fighting a very good rearguard action', but 11 days later the Germans were forced to seek an armistice.

(BOTTOM LEFT) A German casualty. At the beginning of November the Germans still had 3.5 million men on the Western Front. Over the previous seven months it had lost more than 1.2 million, many of its most experienced men who had been creamed off into the Stormtroops.

(ABOVE) Field Marshal Hindenburg inspecting the wounded. By mid-October he was aware that the demoralization of the army was such that total collapse was only a matter of time. On 26 October, Ludendorff, the commander on the Western Front, resigned.

FINALLY, ON THE
ELEVENTH HOUR, OF
THE ELEVENTH DAY,
OF THE ELEVENTH
MONTH THE GUNS FELL
SILENT.

(ABOVE) US troops cheering
the news of the armistice.

(TOP AND BOTTOM RIGHT)
Crowds in New York flock on
to the streets to celebrate peace.

I had a future. . . . There was a
future ahead of me,
something I had not imagined
for some years . . . .

LIEUTENANT R. G. DIVEN:
231 SIEGE BATTERY

THE COMBATANTS NOW TURNED TO THE MASSIVE TASK OF REBUILDING A
WORLD WHICH HAD BEEN TORN APART.

(TOP LEFT) Women of the
Commonwealth War Graves
Commission tending the first
cemetery in northern France.
During the war, the British
Empire suffered almost
1 million dead, Austria-
Hungary 1.29 million, France
1.36 million, Germany 1.8
million and Russia 1.7 million.

(BOTTOM LEFT) French
civilians returning to their
shattered village. Tens of
thousands had been displaced
and the majority of buildings
anywhere near the front
ruined. The horrors it had
suffered made France in
particular determined that it
should never fight another war.

(ABOVE) German troops still
with their guns and uniforms in
Berlin. The fact that much of
the German army was allowed
to march back across the Rhine
without being disarmed gave
rise to the myth that it was a
'stab in the back' by socialist
politicians that had defeated it,
rather than the Allies.

(TOP AND BOTTOM LEFT)
Street fighting and unrest in
Munich in 1919. Germany
swiftly descended into chaos.
The government of the Weimar
Republic never had widespread
public support and resentment
at the peace terms imposed by
the Allies gave impetus to
extremists who were
determined to restore Germany
to its 'rightful' place in the world.

(ABOVE) Italian Fascists
marching in Rome shortly after
Mussolini's seizure of power in
1921. His ultra-nationalistic
and authoritarian ideology
seemed to suggest a way out of
the chaos which had engulfed
many countries. His techniques
were to be copied by a much
more sinister figure in
Germany who was just starting
out as a minor political leader.

FURTHER READING

GENERAL
John Keegan, *The First World War* (Hutchinson, 1998)
A.J.P. Taylor, *World War I: An Illustrated History* (Penguin, 1966)
John Terraine, *White Heat: The New Warfare 1914–18* (Sidgwick & Jackson, 1982)

CHAPTER 1: The World Goes to War
Malcolm Brown, *Tommy Goes to War* (Everyman, 1978)
John Keegan, *The Opening Moves: August 1914* (Macmillan, 1973)
John Terraine, *Mons: The Retreat to Victory* (Batsford, 1960)
Barbara Tuchman, *The Guns of August* (Constable & Robinson, 2000)

CHAPTER 2: Blood and Mud
Malcolm Brown, *The Imperial War Museum Book of the Somme* (Sidgwick & Jackson, 1996)
Malcolm Brown, *The Imperial War Museum Book of the Western Front* (Sidgwick & Jackson, 1993)
Alistair Horne, *The Price of Glory, Verdun 1916* (Penguin, 1964)
Lyn Macdonald, *1915: The Death of Innocence* (Headline, 1993)
Lyn Macdonald, *They Called It Passchendaele* (Michael Joseph, 1978)
Charles Messenger, *Trench Fighting 1914–18* (Ballantine, 1973)
Ian Passingham, *Pillars of Fire: The Battles of Messines Ridge* (Sutton Publishing, 1998)
Gary Sheffield, *The Somme* (Weidenfeld & Nicolson, 2003)
John Terraine, *The Western Front 1914–18* (Arrow Books, 1970)

CHAPTER 3: Aces High
Alan Clark, *Aces High: War in the Air Over the Western Front, 1914–18* (Weidenfeld & Nicolson, 1973)
Peter Hart and Nigel Steel, *Tumult in the Clouds: the British Experience of War in the Air 1914–18* (Hodder & Stoughton, 1997)
Peter Kilduff, *Richthofen: Beyond the Legend of the Red Baron* (John Wiley & Sons, 1994)
Terry C. Treadwell and Alan C. Wood, *The First Air War, The Pictorial History 1914–19* (Brassey's UK, 1996)

CHAPTER 4: Battle Fleets and U-Boats
Peter Hart and Nigel Steel, *Jutland, 1916: Death in the Grey Wastes* (Weidenfeld & Nicolson, 2003)
John Terraine, *Business in Great Waters: the U-boat Wars 1916–45* (Pen & Sword/Leo Cooper, 1989)

CHAPTER 5: War of the Eagles
Peter Hart and Nigel Steel, *Defeat at Gallipoli* (Macmillan, 1994)
Norman Stone, *The Eastern Front: 1914–17* (Hodder, 1975)

CHAPTER 6: War to End All War?
Malcolm Brown, *The Imperial War Museum Book of 1918* (Pan, 1999)
Lyn Macdonald, *To the Last Man 1918* (Penguin, 1999)
Martin Middlebrook, *The Kaiser's Battle, 21 March 1918* (Viking, 1978)
John Terraine, *1918: The Year of Victory* (Sidgwick & Jackson, 1978)

INDEX

Page numbers in *italic* indicate photographs

British H Type 134
use in coastal waters 128
use in underground tunnels 52,
  78–9
'Miracle of the Marne' 20, *59*
Montenegro 158, 195
Morocco, disputes over 15
Moscow, bodies of the fallen are
  paraded through the streets *181*
motor vehicles, British use of *72*
munitions factories *47*, *59*

Napoleon III, Emperor 14
naval warfare 1914–1918 127–53
navies, use of aircraft 95–7
New Zealand navy 128
New Zealand, troops contribution 61
Nicholas II, Tsar 13, 155
  and family *24*, *185*
  and his army *25*
  end of the Russian monarchy 1917
    160
  personal command of Russian
    armies 1915 158
  Tsar and Tsarevitch inspect
    Cossack officers *180*
Nicholas, Grand Duke 155, 156, 157
Nivelle, General Robert 50, 51, *76*
North Sea, Battle of Dogger Bank
  1915 129–30, 132

observation balloons, tethered 92,
  116, *117*
October Revolution in Russia
  159–65
Ottoman Empire 15, 16, 190, 194

Pacific, war in 23
parachutes, use of 92, 115, 116
Paris
  early fighting around 20
  street scene *29*
  taxis take troops to the front *59*
Paris Peace Conference 1919 194–5
Passchendaele ridge, battle for 52
peace treaties, signing at Versailles
  1919 195
Pershing, General John ('Black
  Jack') *86*, *87*, 188
Pétain, General 51, *77*
Petrograd *see* St Petersburg
Philippines 14
pilots
  American *112*, *113*
  French *108*, *110*

German *110*, *111*
life expectancy 109
Royal Flying Corps *109*
Poland 164, 190, 194, 196
Polish salient, attempts to open
  Eastern Front 21
Princip, Gavril 17
  after shooting the Archduke 1914 *30*
Prussia
  defeat of Austro-Hungary in 1866 13
  defeat of France 1870 14
Przemysl fortress, fighting for 156, 157
Puerto Rico 14

Q-ships 133, *150*

Race to the Sea 45
radio
  air-to-ground 92
  use by Russians in 1914 22
radio direction-finding, to detect
  U-boats 134
radio signals, intercepted 129, 131,
  156
radio telegraph operators *118*
Rasputin, Grigori 160
reconnaissance, from the air 91, 92
Red Baron *see* Richthofen, Baron
  Manfred von
Richthofen, Baron Manfred von (the
  Red Baron) 91, 93, *110*, *111*
Rickenbacker, Eddie *113*
Riga, capture by Germans 162
Romania 159, 164
Royal Air Force, creation of 100
Royal Flying Corps 92, 100
Royal Naval Air Service 96, 97, 98,
  99, 100
Royal Navy 14
  use of airships *122*
Royal Navy Grand Fleet 128, 131,
  143, *144*, *145*
Royal Navy Mediterranean Fleet 128
Rules of War 140
Russia
  1905 Revolution 15
  agitator distributing leaflets *178*
  Baltic fleet 128
  Black Sea fleet 128
  colonial rivalry with Japan 15
  defeat at Tsushima Straits 1905 15
  formal exit from the war 1918 187
  October 1917 revolution 53,
    159–65
  pact with France 1894 16

peace treaty with Central Powers
  164
Petrograd Soviet of Workers' and
  Soldiers' Deputies 1917 160
Provisional Government 1917
  160–3
Red armies 192–3
  support for Slavs in the Balkans 16,
    18
  White armies 192–3
Russian Army
  attack on East Prussia 1914 21–2
  campaign in the Caucasus 171
  conscripts being called up in 1916 *179*
  fighting on the Eastern Front 155,
    156–9, 161
  in 1914 21
  troops *166*, *167*, *171*
Russian Civil War 165, 192–3
Russian Empire 13
Russian Navy, 1916 mutinies 159–60
Russian peasant life in 1914 *25*
Russian Poland, attack by Austro-
  Hungary 1914 21
Russian prisoners, Tannenberg *43*

Sarajevo, assassination in 1914 17
Scapa Flow 128, 131
Scheer, Admiral Reinhard von
  130–1
Schlieffen, Count Alfred von
  (Schlieffen Plan) 18–19, 20
Serbia
  as part of Yugoslavia 195
  events leading to war 16–18
  fighting on the Eastern Front 155,
    158
ships
  armoured cruisers 127
  battle-cruisers 127–8
  battleship *Svent Istvan* sinking *153*
  battleships 15–16, 127, *144*, *145*
  British *Acasta*-class destroyer *148*
  British B-class submarine loading a
    torpedo *140*
  British submarines 128
  cruisers 127
  dreadnought 127, 137, 138
  German *Nassau*-class dreadnought
    159
  German U-boats 128
  HMS *Argus* 125
  HMS *Barham* 145
  HMS *Dreadnought* 15, 127, 137, *139*
  HMS *Erebus* 152

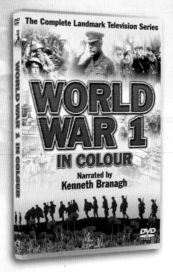
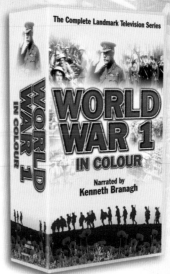